How Washington Lost His Birthday and Other Masonic Essays

Also from Westphalia Press
westphaliapress.org

How Washington Lost His Birthday and Other Masonic Essays

Gaston Lichtenstein's
How George Washington Lost His Birthday

Introduced and Edited by Guillermo De Los Reyes

WESTPHALIA PRESS
An imprint of the Policy Studies Organization

How Washington Lost His Birthday
and Other Masonic Essays
Gaston Lichtenstein's *George Washington's Lost Birthday*

Westphalia Press
An imprint of Policy Studies Organization
dgutierrezs@ipsonet.org

For information:
Westphalia Press
1527 New Hampshire Ave., N.W.
Washington, D.C. 20036

ISBN-13: 978-1935907206
ISBN-10: 1935907204

Cover design by Taillefer Long at Illuminated Stories:
www.illuminatedstories.com

Updated material and comments on this edition can be found at the Westphalia Press website: westphaliapress.org

Dedicated to John Cooper,
fellow scholar of the Craft

GASTON LICHTENSTEIN AS ANTIQUARIAN
PREFACE TO THE NEW EDITION

George Lichtenstein (1879-1954) was an antiquarian with a particular interest in Freemasonry. Now, some take exception if they are labeled as antiquarians, because they feel that the difference between an antiquarian and a historian is that the former in not scientific in approach. But another way to look at it is that an antiquarian, and Lichtenstein is no exception, is characterized by an enormous appetite for all sorts of subjects. If it were not for antiquarians there is a great deal we would not know, although whether we want to know it is another matter.

In any event, besides explaining the troubles caused by the calendar changes of the eighteenth century, and the curious Masonic daylight lodges, we also are given in this volume a small excursion into Mexican War history and an appreciation of Andrew Johnson.

All of this perhaps goes to show that antiquarian authors need to be introduced to antiquarian readers, which perhaps this book can facilitate.

Guillermo De Los Reyes
University of Houston

E

F

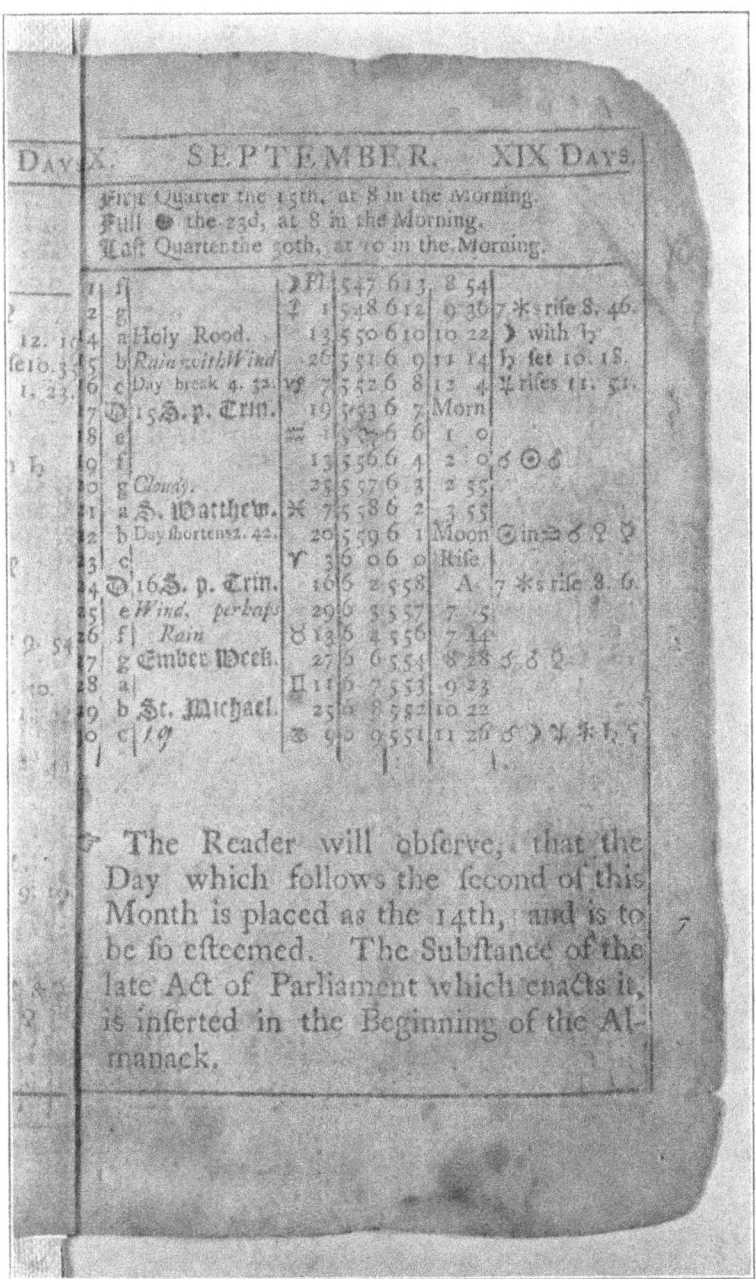

| Days X. | SEPTEMBER. | XIX Days. |

First Quarter the 15th, at 8 in the Morning.
Full ● the 23d, at 8 in the Morning.
Last Quarter the 30th, at 10 in the Morning.

	1	f		♊ Pl.	547 613	8 54	
	2	g		♋ 1	548 612	9 36	7 ✳ rise 8. 46.
12. 1	14	a	Holy Rood.	13	550 610	10 22	☽ with ♄
fe 10.	15	b	Rain with Wind	26	551 6 9	11 14	♄ set 10. 18.
1. 23	16	c	Day break 4. 32	♑ 7	552 6 8	12 4	♃ rises 11. 51.
	17	☽ 15 S. p. Trin.	19	553 6 7	Morn		
	18	e		♒	554 6 6	1 0	
	19	f		13	556 6 4	2 0 ☌ ☉ ☾	
	20	g	Cloudy.	25	557 6 3	2 55	
	21	a	S. Matthew.	♓ 7	558 6 2	3 55	
	22	b	Day shortens 2. 42.	20	559 6 1	Moon ☉ in ♎ ☌ ♀ ☿	
	23	c		♈ 3	6 0 6 0	Rise	
	24	☽ 16 S. p. Trin.	16	2 558	A. 7 ✳ rise 8. 6.		
	25	e	Wind, perhaps	29	3 557	7 5	
	26	f	Rain	♉ 13	4 556	7 14	
	27	g	Ember Week.	27	6 554	8 28 ☌ ☌ ☿	
	28	a		♊ 11	7 553	9 23	
	29	b	St. Michael	25	8 552	10 22	
	30	c	19	♋ 9	9 551	11 20 ☌ ☽ ♃ ✳ ♄	

☞ The Reader will observe, that the Day which follows the second of this Month is placed as the 14th, and is to be so esteemed. The Substance of the late Act of Parliament which enacts it, is inserted in the Beginning of the Almanack.

FROM A VIRGINIA ALMANAC FOR 1752
It will be noted the eleven days dropped are from the 3d to 13th, inclusive.

GEORGE WASHINGTON'S
LOST BIRTHDAY

HISTORY OF MERIDIAN LODGE

ALSO OTHER ARTICLES
WRITTEN AT VARIOUS TIMES

By Gaston Lichtenstein

PREFACE

Before 1752, February stood near the foot of the Calendar. Since January 1st and New Year's Day now seem interchangeable terms, it will be difficult for Twentieth Century minds to appreciate the momentous changes which took place, when the New Style was adopted.

William Hunter, of Williamsburg, printed an Almanac for 1752, setting forth on pages two and three how New Year's Day would be moved from March 25th to January 1st and other alterations. Owing to the state of the paper, photographic reproduction was inadvisable. Fortunately, the month of September (with its missing eleven days) yielded successfully to the camera.

' Thanks are due to Dr. H. R. McIlwaine, State Librarian, for permission to photograph any part of the Virginia Almanac, and to his Secretary, Miss Rose Goode, for facilitating the work. To Wilmer L. Hall, Assistant State Librarian, the writer is indebted for calling attention to its availability.

Passing from years to hours, it is timely to mention that there are few "daylight" lodges in the United States. They exist for the benefit of those Masons, who cannot attend night meetings. New York City's largest Blue Lodge, St. Cecile, draws a considerable number of members from the metropolitan dailies, from musicians and from the theatrical profession. Richmond's unique organization, Meridian Lodge, can add three different classes: preachers, physicians, and railroad men.

J. G. Hankins, editor of the *Virginia Masonic Journal,* graciously allowed use of all material in his possession. The likenesses of Washington the Mason, Charles A. Nesbitt, Grand Secretary, and Rev. Frank T. Mc-Faden, Master of two lodges simultaneously, were borrowed from him.

Being a native of Tarboro, on Tar River, the writer feels himself superlatively entitled to the designation of Tarheel. He will offer no other reason for including North Carolina history, biography and genealogy. He admits that a residence of many years on the north bank of the James makes him look like a pure Richmonder. He is a descendant, on both sides, from Virginians—which ought to help some.

Finally, the subscribers deserve special mention. Without their assistance this book would be only a dream.

CONTENTS

GEORGE WASHINGTON'S
LOST BIRTHDAY

Members of the Masonic fraternity have often discussed not only by the spoken word but in print, Washington's affiliation with the oldest and probably best known fraternal order in the world. He was initiated on November 4, 1752. According to the New Style Calendar, he would have been less than twenty-one years of age. However, an examination of the facts discloses a curious situation.

First of all, George Washington was born during the year 1731. It is rather well known that he saw the light of day on February 11th. Historians may write it February 22, 1732, to simplify the subject; but they leave unexplained an interesting matter. Changing from the Old Style to the New Style did more to the Calendar than affect only eleven days, as is commonly supposed.

Before 1752, England began her year on March 25th. Virginians are so accustomed to think of January 1st as New Year's Day that it may slightly shock them to learn how comparatively recent has been the observance of the latter date by their Anglo-Saxon ancestors. Of course, the American Colonies observed English law in this respect.

Popular prejudice in Great Britain successfully opposed for a long time adoption of the New Style Calendar. Excepting Scotland, where January 1st was adopted for New Year's Day, as far back as 1600, the British maintained their traditional conservatism. Finally, they saw the inconvenience of using a different date from the one employed by a large part of Europe.

Through the courtesy of W. W. Scott, Law Librarian of Virginia, the following copy of the law, upon which this article has been based, is reproduced for the light it will shed. It deserves a careful reading. Few persons realize what a change was effected through alteration of the Calendar. As the Act states, "divers Inconveniences" resulted from beginning the year on the 25th of March. Without further ado, the law will tell its own tale:

"Act of British Parliament for Regulating the Commencement of the Year; and for Correcting the Calendar now in Use."

"Whereas, the legal Supputation of the Year of our Lord in that Part of Great Britain called England, according to which the Year beginneth on the twenty-fifth day of March, hath been found by Experience to be attended with divers Inconveniences, not only as it differs from the Usage of neighboring Nations,

WASHINGTON, THE MASON

but also from the legal Method of Computation in that part of Great Britain called Scotland, and from the common Usage throughout the whole Kingdom, and thereby frequent Mistakes are occasioned in the Dates of Deeds, and other Writings, and Disputes arise therefrom: And whereas, the Calendar now in Use throughout all his Majesty's British Dominions, commonly called the Julian Calendar, hath been discovered to be erroneous, by Means whereof the Vernal or Spring Equinox, which at the Time of the General Council of Nice, in the Year of our Lord three hundred and twenty-five, happened on or about the twenty-first day of March, now happens on the ninth or tenth Day of the same Month; and the said Error is still increasing, and if not remedied, would, in Process of Time, occasion the several Equinoxes and Solstices to fall at very different Times in the Civil Year from what they formerly did, which might tend to mislead Persons ignorant of the said Alteration: And whereas, a method of correcting the Calendar in such Manner, as that the Equinoxes and Solstices may for the future fall nearly on the same nominal Days, on which the same happened at the Time of the said General Council, hath been received and established, and is now generally practised by about all other Nations of Europe: And whereas, it will be of general Convenience to Merchants, and other

Persons corresponding with other Nations and Countries, and tend to prevent Mistakes and Disputes in or concerning the Dates of Letters, and Accounts, if the like Correction be received and established in His Majesty's Dominions."

"May it therefore please your Majesty, that it may be enacted, and be it enacted by the King's Most Excellent Majesty, by and with the Advice and Consent of the Lords Spiritual and Temporal, and Commons, in this present Parliament assembled, and by the Authority of the same, That in and throughout all His Majesty's Dominions and Countries in Europe, Asia, Africa and America, belonging or subject to the Crown of Great Britain, the said Supputation, according to which the Year of Our Lord beginneth, on the twenty-fifth Day of March, shall not be made use of from and after the last Day of December, one thousand seven hundred and fifty-one; and that the first Day of January next following the said last Day of December shall be reckoned, taken, deemed and accounted to be the first Day of the Year of our Lord one thousand seven hundred and fifty-two; and the first Day of January which shall happen next after the said first Day of January, one thousand seven hundred and fifty-two, shall be reckoned, taken, deemed and accounted to be the first Day of the year of our Lord one thousand seven hundred and fifty-three; and so on, from Time to Time, the first Day of January in every Year, which shall happen in time to come, shall be reckoned, taken, deemed and accounted to be the first Day of the Year; and that each New Year shall accordingly commence, and begin to be reckoned, from the first Day of every such Month of January next preceding the twenty-fifth Day of March, on which such Year would, according to the present Supputation, have begun or commenced," etc.

From the above it will be observed that the year 1751 ended on December 31st and that, instead of March 25th continuing as New Year's Day, the Act expressly states, "and that the first Day of January next following the said last Day of December shall be reckoned, taken, deemed and accounted to be the first Day of the Year of our Lord one thousand seven hundred and fifty-two."

Therefore, 1751 had no months of January, February, and part of March.

Is it not easy to see how George Washington lost his twentieth birthday? While his actual age may have been twenty during 1752, it was not so, according to the Calendar. In order to avoid confusion, it was more convenient for all persons, who were born between January 1st and March 25th, to skip a birthday.

Dr. Joseph W. Eggleston, Past Grand Master of Masons in Virginia, has given thought to the subject and says that upon Washington's coffin plate, is inscribed: "Aet. 68." This would tend to prove loss of a birthday. From 1732 to 1799, the dates usually accepted, one must figure sixty-seven years. However, adding the lost birthday to the age of the Father of his Country, not only makes him twenty-one, when he was initiated as a Mason, but also explains the inscription upon his coffin plate.—*Reprinted by permission from the April, 1923, Sons of the Revolution Magazine.*

A HISTORY OF RICHMOND'S
DAYLIGHT LODGE

Although Meridian Lodge is less than twenty-one years old, important facts in regard to its organization will soon be lost, if the history does not find its way to a printed page. Right Worshipful Charles A. Nesbitt, the only living charter member who knows all the attendant circumstances, has given to the writer the following statement:

"I read in the Masonic Standard of New York City that there was a 'daylight' lodge in said city and I thought it would be well to have one in Richmond for the benefit of the members of the Craft who were occupied at night. Having mentioned this fact to Brother O. M. Driscoll, then a member of No. 11, who thought the idea a good one, I obtained the petition for a dispensation for a new lodge to meet in this city in the daytime. I was the first signer to said petition and Brother Driscoll was the second."

In connection with the above, it should be put upon record that Brother Nesbitt, first secretary of Meridian Lodge, was the "father" of 207 (Lodge of Strict Observance); also he took the initiative in organizing the various Scottish Rite bodies of the city.

According to the original minutes, "the first communication of Meridian Lodge was held at the Masonic Temple, Richmond, Va., Monday, October 26th, A. L. 5903, A. D. 1903." After reading the Dispensation of the Grand Master, the original list of members was inscribed upon the minutes. They appear as follows:

Wor. Charles A. Nesbitt, O. M. Driscoll, Frank A. Christian, William S. Gill, Charles T. Hardwicke, Harry Huber, James C. Drinard, G. A. Sinclair, W. A. Jacob, Felix Iardella, P. Hellstern, T. E. Stratton, William Krause, J. T. Pulling, Wor. W. N. Watkins, E. M. Eppes, Wor. W. J. Lynham, S. B. Drinard, Wor. T. W. McCaw, G. A. Kass, Wor. F. W. Cunningham, I. L. Weinstein, Wor. Hay T. Thornton, G. D. Beazley, Wor. R. T. Bibb, Charles O. Saville, Wor. J. J. English, Jr., S. S. Rosendorf, Wor. H. W. Tyler, John S. Smith, B. F. Tinsley, D. Rosendorf, H. W. O'Keefe, W. F. Drinkard, J. W. Winfree and Isaac Hutzler (36).

Officers elected and installed at this first meeting were: Wor. W. N. Watkins, treasurer; Wor. Charles A. Nesbitt, secretary, who held the position for ten years; Thomas E. Stratton, Senior Deacon; G. D. Beazley,

Junior Deacon; John S. Smith, Tiler, and William Krause, Purveyor.

Wor. Frank W. Cunningham, who acted as Master, served the Lodge in this capacity for three successive terms; the first Senior and Junior Wardens were: O. M. Driscoll and William S. Gill, respectively. Two petitions were presented. D. H. Parrish and Jesse D. Coats (who was the first to be "raised") enjoy the distinction of having been the candidates for the degrees.

No. 284 received its charter December 3, 1903. At a special communication, held Monday, January 11, 1904, thanks were extended to Rt. Wor. Brothers Hawkins, Charleton and Eggleston "for their kindness in being present this afternoon and constituting this Lodge under its charter."

Among the incidents, worthy of preservation, may be mentioned that on June 28, 1909, Brother R. W. Forsyth (at that time rector of St. Paul's Episcopal Church) was initiated, passed and raised. He almost immediately received the appointment of Chaplain. The weather must have made itself conspicuous for, at this communication, a motion prevailed to allow members to appear hereafter at meetings without coats.

On May 23, 1910, Brothers Wilmer, Forsyth and Nesbitt were appointed to draft resolutions as to the death of Brother Edward VII and forward them both to the Grand Master of England and to the widow. At the October meeting a letter of acknowledgment from the Secretary of State for Foreign Affairs of Great Britain was read. The Lodge ordered it framed and hung on the wall of the room.

An invitation from the general contractor of the postoffice in this city was extended to Meridian Lodge, through Wor. Brother Frank W. Cunningham, to lay the cornerstone of that building; which event took place December 17, 1910. It was an affair upon an elaborate scale. A band, under the direction of Brother Joseph C. Kessnich, furnished the music. Orator of the occasion was Brother A. J. Montague, ex-Governor of Virginia.

A programme, preserved by No. 284, gives the Order of Procession as appended:

Mounted Police—Sergeant R. B. Sowell in Command.

Band—Bro. J. C. Kessnich, Musical Director.

Richmond Commandery, No. 2, K. T.

Commandery of St. Andrews, No. 13, K. T.

Meridian Lodge, No. 284.

Tiler with Drawn Sword—Bro. W. J. Lynham.

Stewards, with White Rods—Bro. J. M. Whitfield and Bro. W. B. Mallory.

Master Masons.

CHARLES A. NESBITT, 33° HON.,
Grand Secretary of the Grand Lodge of
Virginia, and "father" of Meridian Lodge,
Ancient Free and Accepted Masons

Past Masters.

Wor. J. L. Beck, with Vessel Containing Corn.

Rt. Wor. B. P. Owen, Jr., with Square.

Rt. Wor. H. L. Hulce, with Level.

Rt. Wor. F. M. Reade, with Plumb.

Wor. O. J. Mallory, with Vessel Containing Wine.

Wor. C. S. Perry, with Vessel Containing Oil.

Wor. W. N. Watkins, Treasurer.

Wor. Chas. A. Nesbitt, Secretary.

Wor. B. T. August, Wor. B. A. Hord, Wor. A. F. Jahnke, Jr., Wor. Jno. B. Welsh, Wor. W. D. Kern, carrying the Five Orders of Architecture.

Wor. J. G. Hankins, carrying Large Light.

Bro. A. L. Winfield, Senior Warden.

Bro. Manfred Call, Junior Warden.

Rt. Wor. O. A. Hawkins, carrying the Holy Bible, Square and Compasses.

Bro. McCaw Tompkins, Stewards, with White Rods.

Supported by Bro. A. H. Flournoy, Wor. O. J. Adams, Wor. L. B. Siegfried, carrying Large Lights.

Bro. Robt. W. Forsyth, Chaplain.

Wor. A. P. Wilmer, carrying Book of Constitutions.

Wor. W. P. Matthews, Master.

Supported by Bro. Geo. W. Lowery, Senior Deacon.

Bro. C. M. Miller, Junior Deacon.

Wor. F. W. Cunningham, Marshal.

Brother Robert W. Forsyth, who had served as Chaplain from the day upon which he received all three degrees, nine days after taking part in the above event, was elected to the office of Senior Deacon. But, this most worthy member of the Craft did not live to enjoy the honor. At the meeting, held February 27, 1911, Wor. W. P. Matthews reported that he had performed the duty committed to him at the last stated communication of this Lodge and that Brother Forsyth expressed his high appreciation of the kind interest shown by the Lodge and his hope of being with us very soon. One month later, resolutions upon the death of Brother Forsyth were ordered to be engrossed and hung upon the wall of the Lodge.

On May 27, 1912, Most Worshipful A. R. Courtney made an interesting talk on Masonry during the War Between the States. He had been a member of an Army Lodge, which fact qualified him to speak authoritatively upon this subject.

Rev. Frank T. McFaden, D. D., probably occupied a position unique in the history of Masonry in the United States. As Master (during 1921), both of Dove and Meridian Lodges, he enjoyed a distinction, which

REV. FRANK T. MCFADEN, D. D.

caused widespread comment. Notwithstanding his pastoral duties, in addition to the work put upon him by two Masonic bodies, he also found time to serve as head of the Rotary Club.

LAYS CORNERSTONE OF MATTHEW F. MAURY MONUMENT

Meridian, No. 284, Richmond's unique noonday meeting Lodge, had charge of laying the cornerstone of the Matthew Fontaine Maury Monument at Monument and Belmont Avenues, in Richmond, on June 22, 1922. The Lodge was selected for the work in compliment to Gaston Lichtenstein,* its chaplain, and one of its most active members, who for eight years has been corresponding secretary of the Matthew Fontaine Maury Association.

The Lodge left the Masonic Temple at 2:30 o'clock by street cars to Mulberry and Broad Streets, where the procession was formed and marched to the monument site.

The order of procession was as follows:

Mounted police.

Richmond Commandery, No. 2, Knights Templar.

Commandery of St. Andrews, No. 13, Knights Templar.

Marshal, Worshipful E. L. Perkins. Tiler, Brother W. C. Lynham. Stewards with rods,

---

*This portion of the article, having been written by the then editor of the Virginia Masonic Journal, explains the recurrence of the compiler's name.

Brother L. A. Crew and Brother G. G. Moss. Master Masons in double order. Past masters in double order. A past master with vessel containing corn, Worshipful George W. Lowery. Three master Masons with—square, Brother N. W. Harding; level, Brother T. H. Isbell; plumb, Brother H. O. Burks. Two past masters with vessels containing oil, Worshipful C. L. Limerick; wine, Worshipful A. H. Flournoy; treasurer, Worshipful H. F. Ryder. Secretary, Brother J. N. Otey. Five master Masons with orders of architecture—Tuscan, Brother J. G. Frasier; Doric, Brother D. H. Harden; Ionic, Brother L. D. Stout; Corinthan, Brother L. H. Watson; Composite, Brother J. C. Bullock. A past master with one large light, Worshipful O. J. Mallory. Senior Warden, Brother J. B. Anderson. Junior Warden, Brother H. M. Thomas. Holy Bible, square and compasses, by Worshipful J. L. Beck, supported by two stewards with white rods, Brothers H. E. Briel and F. H. Herndon. Two large lights, by Right Worshipful Charles A. Nesbitt and Worshipful A. P. Wilmer. Chaplain, Right Worshipful Frank T. McFaden. Choristers, Brothers Norman Call, Maurice L. Tyler, E. R. Dyson and M. A. Dyson. Chairman of Music Committee, T. S. Hiteshew. Book of constitutions, by Worshipful H. M. Cousins. Worshipful master, Worshipful A. T. Skelding. Deacons supporting worshipful master—senior deacon, Brother J. W. W. Valentine; junior deacon, Brother J. C. Lewis.

The order of exercises was as follows:

"America," by the assembly. Proclamation of the marshal, Worshipful E. L. Perkins. The worshipful master informed the officers and members of the nature of the occasion. Prayer, Right Worshipful Frank T. McFaden. Request that the cornerstone be laid according to the ancient usages of freemasonry was made by Gaston Lichtenstein, of Matthew Fontaine Maury Association. Ode. Stone made ready and box deposited. Singing. Grand honors. Singing. Consecration of stone. Distribution of corn of nourishment by worshipful master. Hymn.

Pouring of oil on threshold and on cornerstone. Wine of refreshment, by senior warden. Oil of joy and gladness, by junior warden. Final approval of the stone, by worshipful master. Grand honors. Singing.

Oration, Hon. E. Lee Trinkle, Governor of Virginia, a member of Wytheville Fraternal Lodge, No. 82; introduced by Mrs. Frank Anthony Walke, representing the United Daughters of Confederacy. Oration, Hon. A. B. Chandler; introduced by General Julian S. Carr, commander-in-chief, United Confederate Veterans, who himself was presented by Mrs.

E. E. Moffitt, president of the Maury Association. Oration, Mrs. Livingston Rowe Schuyler,
president-general, Daughters of the Confederacy. Proclamation, Worshipful E. L.
Perkins, Benediction, Brother S. L. Dumville.

Masters of Meridian Lodge, since its organization, have been: Frank W. Cunningham
(1904-5-6), J. L. Beck (1907), O. J. Mallory
(1908), C. S. Perry (1909), W. P. Matthews
(1910), Manfred Call (1911), A. L. Winfield
(1912), G. W. Lowery (1913), H. F. Ryder
(1914), A. H. Flournoy (1915), Marshall L.
Boyle, Sr. (1916), H. M. Cousins (1917),
Wm. Bernstein (1918), C. L. Limerick (1919),
Victor St. John Vaughan (1920), Frank T.
McFaden (1921), A. T. Skelding (1922), and
James B. Anderson (1923).

Officers for 1924: Hunter McGuire Thomas,
worshipful master; John C. Lewis, senior
warden; D. Humphrey Harden, junior warden; Wor. Harrison F. Ryder, treasurer; Wor.
V. St. John Vaughan, secretary; Joseph N.
Otey, senior deacon; C. Murray Moncure,
junior deacon; W. L. Bragg and W. J. Scott,
stewards; Rt. Wor. Charles A. Nesbitt, Wor.
James L. Beck, Wor. John J. Gravatt, Gaston
Lichtenstein, Wor. O. J. Mallory, chaplains;
W. C. Lynham (51), tiler; A. W. Baker,
purveyor.

FRAGMENTS OF VIRGINIA
MASONIC HISTORY

In the Grand Lodge library, located in the Masonic Temple at Richmond, there is a set of the Freemasons Monthly Magazine. This Massachusetts publication, edited by the then Grand Secretary of that State, contains many items of interest to Virginians. It will be impossible, in an article of this scope, to do more than select a few of them.

On July 1, 1843, there appeared the following communication from the Grand Lecturer of the Grand Lodge of Ohio:

"We have in Ohio, two venerable brethren whose names I should be pleased to see published in your magazine. The first is Captain Hugh Maloy, aged about 93, now living in or near Bethel, Clermont county. He was initiated in the year 1782, in General Washington's markee. *General Washington presided in person, and performed the initiating ceremonies.* The other is Brother J. McLane, now in his *one hundred and seventh year!* His diploma is dated, I think, in the year 1762. He has consequently been a Mason *eighty-one years!* In his hundred and fourth year, he received, in a Chapter at Maysville, Ky., the several degrees conferred therein!"

Charlestown, on May 16, 1844, was the scene of a celebration, which the Massachusetts magazine devotes two pages to. After exercises in the town itself, a procession formed and proceeded three miles out to the Cave, where it is said George Washington held the first lodge of Masons ever assembled west of the Blue Ridge. The Cave was illuminated for the occasion; "beautifully," so it is written. About 150 of the Craft, two companies of volunteers, a band of music and a large number of citizens entered the "subterraneous excavation." More than half an hour was spent in exploring the different apartments of this natural curiosity.

On September 1, 1858, the Richmond Dispatch was honored by the Boston publication with special mention because the Virginia, newspaper had referred to social intercourse between citizens of various parts of the country as the best means of breaking down sectionalism and reviving declining national sentiment. In the light of subsequent events, just a few years later, the remarks of the Dispatch ought to prove exceptionally interesting as they show the editor's attitude toward the fire-eaters of both sections:

"The Knights Templar of this city are about extending an invitation to the De Molay

Encampment, of Boston, to visit the capital of the Old Dominion, at their pleasure, and we have no doubt that the invitation will be accepted, and that we shall have the Boston Masons in our midst in the course of the next year. Our Masons may not be able to give their visiting Brethren all the delicacies of the sea, nor can they afford them excursions by water, such as they enjoyed in June last; but they can take them into the mountains of Virginia and show them some of the rarest scenery to be found in the Union, and at the same time spread before them such substantials as will not prove distasteful to hungry palates. And, more than all, they can give them an Old Virginia welcome, that will do more to allay sectional strife, and bring about Brotherly Love, and love for the Union, than all the buncombe speeches to be made by Southern and Northern fire-eaters in the next twenty years to come. The people of both sections have only to know, to appreciate each other, and in no way can they so easily become acquainted as by frequent intercourse, by seeing one another at their firesides, and by witnessing the practical workings of the institutions of each section. Virginia and Massachusetts have stood shoulder to shoulder in the hours of peril, and if the people are left to the guidance of their own sound judgments, they will again become united as a band of

Brethren, defending the rights and redressing the wrongs of each other."

While the War Between the States was raging, George Gibbs contributed an article to the Freemasons' Magazine, in which he made the following statement:

"It may be added that a full length statue of Washington in Masonic dress was executed by Powers just before the rebellion [sic], and was designed to be erected at Fredericksburg. It never was set up, however, and is now concealed somewhere at the South."

An Historical Sketch of Fredericksburg Lodge, No. 4, A., F. and A. M., compiled in 1890 by S. J. Quinn, afterwards Grand Master of Masons in Virginia, 1907-08, has this to say of the statue:

"In 1852 the lodge conceived the idea of erecting in this place a Washington Masonic monument. As to what that monument was to consist of, does not appear from any record we can discover, to be well defined. As far as we are able to judge, it was to be a temple with a life-size statue of Washington placed in the the vestibule. The committee made appeals to the Grand Lodge of Virginia and to many of the subordinate lodges, and received liberal donations. The Grand Lodge strongly endorsed the movement, made it a liberal contribution and raised a committee consisting of five past grand masters, which should urge the subordinate lodges in the State to aid in the effort, and also to open correspondence with the grand and subordinate lodges of other States, urge them to aid in the enterprise and thus insure success in the undertaking. With the money subscribed and paid in, a life-size marble statue of Washington, in Masonic regalia, was ordered from Mr. Powers, a Virginia artist, then residing in Rome. This statue was completed, and reached Fredericksburg by the last steamer that came up the Rappahannock River before it was closed to navigation by the Federal authorities at the beginning of the war. It was placed on public exhibition and large numbers of persons inspected it, and the best judges pronounced it to be one of the finest pieces of statuary seen in this country. During the war it was placed in the stone house on Water Street, near the free bridge, and remained there until the summer of 1863, when it was taken to Richmond for safekeeping, and perished in the terrible conflagration that followed the evacuation of that city by the Confederate forces on the 3rd of April, 1865. It is more than likely that had not the war come on, which stopped all efforts in behalf of the monument, it would have been erected and would have proved the pride of the Masonic fraternity of this country."

ST. JOHN'S CHURCH AND ITS RECTOR, ALEXANDER WATSON WEDDELL

One of the most historic structures in the United States is St. John's Church, located in Richmond, Virginia, for it was there that Patrick Henry uttered these memorable words, "Give me liberty, or give me death!"

Tourists, irrespective of section, North, South, East and West reverently visit the sacred spot where the growing spark of Freedom was made to glow with superlative intensity.

As a pupil at Hughes High School in Cincinnati, Ohio, I remember how earnestly the embryo orators would declaim from the rostrum selections from their favorite orations and it did my Southern heart good to hear often the immortal words of the famous Virginian, voluntarily chosen and ardently uttered.

On a lofty eminence, overlooking the old town along the northern bank of the James, was erected a sacred edifice in 1741 and people, gazing upward, would speak of the church "on the hill," whence the name Church Hill, applied at the present time to that part of Richmond contiguous to the Church. Recently, I had occasion to act as guide to a gentleman from New York. We visited St. John's, saw where Patrick Henry stood, were shown the baptismal font, a relic of colonial days and used at Curle's Neck Church long before St. John's was built, had the oldest grave pointed out, also the final resting place of Royal Governor Page, and listened to an extended discourse on Miss Van Lew, whose mansion nearby sheltered Northern soldiers during the War Between the States.

Two strangers, who were in the edifice at the same time, asked me why the Convention of 1775 met in a church.

Williamsburg, the capital, was unsafe as a meeting place on account of the hostility of Governor Dunmore, and the patriotic vestry of Richmond having offered what was probably the largest building in town, the Convention graciously accepted.

On July 30, 1619, the first legislative body that ever assembled in America met in the old church at Jamestown. Therefore, at the outset, a precedent was established for the meeting of a political body in a house of worship.

Parenthetically, it may be remarked that the initial General Assembly sat with their hats on, following the custom of the English lower branch.

Edmund Randolph, who was one of the

vestry, and an eye-witness of the Convention of 1775, has left an account of the scene.

On July 17, 1775, the Convention assembled again in St. John's and this session busied itself with organization of the troops and the adoption of further war measures.

Towards the close of the Revolution the venerable building was desecrated by the soldiers of Benedict Arnold.

No more sincere Thanksgiving services were held in churches throughout America than those within the walls of St. John's, when independence had been assured.

Since that time the civil history of the United States has been impressed with the names of many of its long roll of vestrymen.

Prominently placed, near the present main entrance, a monument towers above the headstones of a former generation, and tourists, who pause for a while, are impelled to read the following inscription:

REV^d ALEX^r WEDDELL, D. D.,
Rector of St. John's Church,
Born at Tarboro, North Carolina,
May 20th, 1841,
Died at Richmond, Va., December 6th, 1883.

J. Staunton Moore, who has compiled a large mass of history relating to the old Parish, writes that he was a frequent attendant at the services held by Alexander W. Weddell, and, although not a communicant at that time, he had the pleasure of Dr. Weddell's acquaintance and enjoyed his friendship as a man and brother Mason for several years before his death; also, he had discussed with him freely in a friendly and social way many doubts that beset and perplexed him on religious matters, and that many sermons had been preached at him.

To continue in the compiler's own words: "Dr. Weddell impressed the writer as being liberal, broad-minded, free from cant and hypocrisy. Plain, simple and unaffected, devoid of slang and free from technical terms. He formed his opinions not in the academic schools, but from practical experience—from actual contact with men. His horizon of thought was bounded by no narrow limits; he thoroughly understood human nature. He did not look down upon humanity from an exalted pedestal. He took mankind as he found it, not as he thought it should be. He had familiarized himself with man's nature, 'in the tented field' as a Confederate soldier; he knew its capacities, its aspirations, its fallibilities. He exercised patience, temperance and moderation to a very rare degree. He was never pessimistic in his religious views, or dogmatic in his discourse or self-conceited in his opinions. A beautiful optimism pervaded his thoughts and breathes in his utterances. A wonderful patience and submission during his lingering illness pervaded his conversation, and governed his actions. Many a time has the writer on the way to his home taken him 'up the hill' in his buggy, when scarcely able to walk, yet still trying to perform his appointed duties. Nature cast him in an heroic mold, not only physically, but endowed him mentally with those graceful virtues calculated to win human hearts, and enshrined his soul in those lovely traits of character that endeared him to all who knew him."

"The restoration, aye, it may be truthfully said, the resurrection of St. John's Church is due to the strenuous efforts and consecrated labors of Dr. Weddell. When he took charge in 1875 there were but 118 communicants. By his earnest zeal, his affability, his sincere piety, he increased the number to 221, the membership continuing to increase yearly until he rested from his labors, adding during the eight years of·his ministerial work 506 communicants and presenting for confirmation 243, the largest increase, up to that time, in the annals of the Church, since its foundation. But St. John's Church for the past forty years has been peculiarly a church of transition. The constant change of the personnel of the congregation has been remarkable, and probably unparalleled in Church history. The tendency to 'move up town' by the residents of the Old Hill as the city grows westward has been going on from year to year, thus causing a shifting membership—here today, gone tomorrow! The tale is told in 'mournful numbers' as the words 'removed or transferred' appear opposite names on the communicant list."

Alexander W. Weddell, a native of Edgecombe county, was the son of James Weddell, who, in early youth, came to this country from Scotland and settled in Eastern North Carolina, where with small means he commenced business. Through genuine worth and persistent effort he secured success and commanded the respect and esteem of all who knew him. As an honest, reliable merchant and a gentleman in social life, he exemplified the strong, positive traits of Scotch character. He married Miss Margaret Ward, of Tarboro, N. C., the union of which was blessed with three sons, John, Alexander W. and Virginius. When his boys were very young, Mr. Weddell moved with his family to Petersburg. At the outbreak of the War Between the States, all three of the young men, who had grown up amid the most favorable surroundings and gave promise of a future life of usefulness, enlisted in the Confederate Army. John, the eldest, was killed at Chancellorsville, and Virginius, the youngest, died of injuries sustained by the falling of a limb which had been torn from a tree overhead, during the course of an engagement at Malvern Hill, when his company was supporting a Confederate battery.

The second son, Alexander W., was first lieutenant of Company G, Forty-first Virginia Regiment. Later on, he was detached to serve in the signal corps, and read the cipher dispatches received by President Davis. Having fortunately passed through the entire struggle without accident, he entered the dry goods business in Petersburg. He desired to enter a profession and, having been advised by friends to choose the ministry in preference to the law, as personally he was undecided, Mr. Weddell left commercial life and in 1868 became a member of the Middle class of the Theological Seminary at Alexandria. Both before and after he entered the ministry, he contributed frequently to the press. Some of the most humorous writings that ever appeared in the Richmond and Petersburg papers were products of his pen.

While living in Petersburg, immediately after the war, he took an active interest in church affairs. Although a layman, he worked as zealously for the upbuilding of Grace Church as if he had been a minister. He did not look down upon humanity; in fact, he was the right-hand man of the rector and largely due to his labors may be attributed the erection of the edifice in which the members of that congregation worshipped subsequent to the surrender.

Being deeply interested in the religious and moral welfare of the negroes, who had just been emancipated, Alexander W. Weddell set to work with Rev. Robert A. Gibson, in the fall of 1865, by opening a Sunday school for colored children in the basement of Grace Church. From a small beginning the movement gradually grew until, with the aid of others, the results were greatly gratifying, one of which was St. Stephen's colored Episcopal Church and Normal School at Petersburg.

Mr. Weddell raised about four thousand dollars for the building and lot, giving one thousand dollars of his own for the lot. When the first church was burned, he provided another place of worship and was so earnest in his efforts that he promised the congregation to let them assemble in his basement if he could not find a suitable meeting place. He read for the congregation and helped the colored people in the Sunday school. For many years he was closely identified with this kind of work and the Bishop of the diocese had great confidence in his judgment; indeed, the colored man owes a debt of gratitude to Alexander W. Weddell.

He was married, on the 31st of January, 1866, to Miss Penelope M. Wright, daughter of

Dr. David Minton Wright, of Norfolk. Being a graduate of Hampden-Sidney College and later a student at the University of Virginia, which institution he left shortly before the outbreak of hostilities, Mr. Weddell was well equipped to begin his studies at a theological seminary. He held his first service as deacon in Emmanuel Church, Harrisonburg, Virginia, Sunday, June 19, 1870. After ordination by Bishop Johns, June 23, 1871, he became rector of the Parish.

In 1875, he was called to St. John's. Of his success in the historic old parish, J. Staunton Moore has told above.

Special permission had to be obtained from the city authorities to allow the body of Alexander W. Weddell to rest in St. John's churchyard. Used for over a hundred years, the cemetery had become dotted with the dead of several generations.

The Episcopal clergy and ministers of other denominations of Richmond were present at the funeral services, conducted by the deceased's old friend, Rev. Dr. Gibson, of Petersburg, who was assisted by Rev. Mr. Burchard, Drs. Dashiell and Peterkin.

The sorrowful assemblage included the Masonic orders of which he was a member (Richmond-Randolph Lodge, No. 19; Royal Arch Chapter, No. 3, and Richmond Commandery, No. 2), and Continental Lodge Knights of

Honor, besides his flock and personal admirers.

Some idea may be formed of the busy life of the beloved rector of St. John's and the severe tax upon his strength when it is remembered that he was often present at the meetings of the various societies, most of which met weekly, conducted in connection with the church.

Four of the five appended organizations were started under Dr. Weddell's ministry: the Brotherhood, devoted to parochial, benevolent and missionary work, the Sisterhood, devoted practically to the same three lines of effort, the Guild, devoted to parochial, charitable work, particularly the clothing of the destitute Sunday school children, the Little Gleaners, devoted especially to missionary work in all departments, and, incidentally, to ministering to the needy in the parish, and the Knights of Temperance, devoted to sobriety among the men and boys.—*From the Tarboro (N. C.) Daily Southerner,, March* 25, 1909.

STATEN ISLAND'S RELICS

To the Editor of The New York Times:

Many Northerners delight in telling Southerners of their slowness. We who live below the Mason and Dixon line are taken to task on account of our carelessness. It is true that much may be done in order to improve our condition, but a recent sight within the bounds of New York State has given me an opportunity to call your attention to an inexcusable neglect on the part of those interested in the preservation of Colonial homes.

Yesterday I had occasion to visit Tottenville, on Staten Island. This village is now within the limits of Greater New York, although its peaceful surroundings suggest only rural pursuits. While on the outskirts of this town it is difficult to realize how near one is to the hurry and congestion of Manhattan.

Let us leave the present and turn back the pages of history! Up to the year 1668 it was a disputed question whether Staten Island belonged to New York or New Jersey. The Duke of York, tired of continual disturbance over this matter, decided that the island would belong to New York if it could be circumnavigated in twenty-four hours; otherwise the land would become a part of New Jersey. A small steamer took me around the island yesterday in somewhat more than four hours, actual time of travel, but, during Colonial days, the trip was an undertaking of considerable size.

Captain Christopher Billopp successfully circumnavigated Staten Island within the period set by the Duke of York, and received for his services a tract of land containing 1,163 acres, on which he built the Manor of Bentley. The old Billopp House, as it is now known, stands on an eminence overlooking Raritan Bay. The cement used came from England and the bricks from Belgium. To see this Colonial structure in a state of decay does not impress a stranger with the up-to-dateness of New York's historical associations.

Do the societies of the Empire State realize that they are neglecting the memory of a man who prevented the possible transfer of Staten Island to New Jersey? They surely have overlooked the treasure (from the standpoint of American history) of a house about 240 years old. The Society for the Preservation of Virginia Antiquities would mark such a structure, if it were found, perchance, in the Old Dominion, and the ladies of the organization would exert their loving care to see that the surrounding land was beautified. With the admirable location, near Raritan Bay, a landscape gardener can do much, and when

Greater New York builds down to Tottenville, the spot should have been amply secured against encroachment, and future generations would be able to look upon a memorial of the time when Indians were· yet upon the scene of the daily life of the settlers.

August 5, 1911.

EDGECOMBE AND THE REVOLUTION*

Shortly before the beginning of the American Revolution, Edmund Burke delivered an address in which he eloquently advocated the conciliation of the colonies by a policy of granting them equal protection and similar privileges to those enjoyed in the mother country. This distinguished British orator, during the course of his mighty effort before Parliament, gave expression to an opinion from which our Northern brethren may dissent. Reference is made to the territory below the Potomac in the following language:

"There is, however, a circumstance attending these Colonies which, in my opinion, fully counterbalances this difference and makes the spirit of liberty still more high and haughty than in those to the northward. It is that in Virginia and the Carolinas they have a vast multitude of *slaves*. Where this is the case in any part of the world, those who are free are by far the most proud and jealous of their freedom. Freedom is to them not only an enjoyment, but a kind of rank and privilege. Not

*Prepared for and read before the North Carolina State Convention of Daughters of the American Revolution, held at Tarboro, November, 1911.

seeing there that freedom as in countries where it is a common blessing, and as broad and general as the air, may be united with much abject toil, with great misery, with all the exterior of servitude, liberty looks amongst them like something that is more noble and liberal. I do not mean, Sir, to commend the superior morality of this sentiment, which has at least as much pride as virtue in it, but I cannot alter the nature of man. The fact is so; and these people of the Southern Colonies are much more strongly and with an higher and more stubborn spirit attached to liberty than those to the northward. Such were all the ancient commonwealths; such were our Gothic ancestors; such, in our days, were the Poles; and such will be all masters of slaves, who are not slaves themselves. In such a people the haughtiness of domination combines with the spirit of freedom, fortifies it and renders it invincible."

Burke's opinion was substantiated in a remarkably brief period after its delivery. Patrick Henry, in Virginia, advocated armed resistance to English oppression almost upon the heels, as it were, of the patriots of Mecklenburg county, North Carolina, who actually declared themselves independent of British authority. These two events are mentioned with the sole object of confirming the Irishman's keen insight into the character of the Southern people. There is no desire to detract from the multitude of patriotic deeds recorded in Northern chronicles. All the colonies united for common defense. Each can relate a story to stir one's blood. But the American struggle for liberty needs to be fully told. Too long has North Carolina hesitated to demand her just place in Revolutionary history!

General accounts of Colonial America devote much space to the happenings in Massachusetts and Virginia. We read how their people protested against the tyranny of George the Third's government. We are willing to accept these records, for the most part, as true. We believe the citizens of Massachusetts and Virginia acted nobly and deserve praise. Yet we feel that the whole truth has not been told. North Carolina's tale also contains incidents of interest. The future American historian will do well to include them in his narrative. He must weigh Edgecombe and Bertie's action in 1737. The revolt did not assume large proportions, but it was sufficient to call forth from the royal Governor special comment, when he made a report to England.

The Quit Rent uprising occurred almost forty years before the outbreak of the American Revolution. Most historians may not see any connection between these two events. Yet a thread of more or less strength does hold together the North Carolina emeute and organized resistance of the colonies, because the former was a distinct protest against the abuse of royal authority. The embryo of discontent had to develop, and many years were required to bring forth a full-grown consciousness. When five hundred men rise for the purpose of rescuing a fellow-citizen, whom they regard as having been unjustly imprisoned, does not that act show dissatisfaction with the established authority?

Consider further these inhabitants of Edgecombe and Bertie. They *curse* the King and utter a great many rebellious speeches. Gabriel Johnston, the Governor, reported to his superiors: "How to quell them I cannot tell if they should attempt an insurrection against the next collection." In this particular case the man arrested made his peace with the General Court at Edenton before the crowd arrived, which circumstance caused the citizens to disperse without doing any harm; but they threatened "the most cruel usage to such persons as durst come to demand any quit rents of them for the future." Johnston delayed a while to comply with the wishes of the people; however he saw that he had determined men to deal with, and ended the unrest by allowing a satisfactory bill to pass the Legislature.

Edgecombe came again into the limelight during the Granville District troubles. Matters went from bad to worse until the people of the affected portion of the colony applied to the Attorney-General for information how to obtain relief. He advised them to follow one of two courses, either to petition the Earl of Granville or to ask the Legislature to consider their grievances. Although William Williams, Edgecombe's Representative, presented a petition to the Assembly in accordance with the advice given, no action was taken. As the Legislature had adjourned without permitting the citizens to obtain any relief, a riotous outbreak took place January 24, 1759. Several months elapsed before calmness prevailed. Although the rioters had no quarrel with the royal Governor, nevertheless seeds of discontent were planted. The men of Granville District contended for their rights.

When the Regulation reached a point where force was necessary to stamp it out, Governor Tryon called upon our county to furnish troops, but the inhabitants showed little enthusiasm. Colonel William Haywood received a letter in which Tryon said if the county did not have men of spirit and ability to comply with his instructions he would endeavor to settle the disturbances without Edgecombe's assistance; however, he trusted the men of the county would not show themselves backward. Rednap Howell, one of the most prominent Regulators, wrote a letter from Halifax on February 16, 1771, to James Hunter. Therein he said: "I found it needless to raise the country, but I am satisfied it could be easily done if the occasion required. However, I have animated the people here to join the Regulation. On Saturday, come two weeks, they are to have a meeting for the purpose. If it once takes start here it will run into the neighboring counties of Edgecombe, Bute and Northampton, and this will undoubtedly facilitate justice to poor Carolina."

Only four years later those who helped a royal governor in his campaign against the Regulators became rebels themselves. The Regulation failed; therefore the participants merited the death of traitors. On the other hand, the Revolution was successful, and rebels again British authority were transformed into patriots.

Because Edgecombe's soil was never the scene of conflict between British troops and Continentals, it must not be inferred that the county presented a calm spectacle. Tarboro's name is often found in the Revolutionary records. But let us first examine the attitude of the people of the county towards independence. When royal authority no longer meant anything to the inhabitants, except the Tories, a committee of safety was formed and its orders were implicitly obeyed.

A few Scotch merchants at the commencement of hostilities lived in Edgecombe, but they preferred remaining subjects to Great Britain. Under the expulsion law they had to leave. The native Tories caused mild disturbances in the county. One of these outbreaks is set forth in the following letter to Governor Caswell from Lieutenant-Colonel Henry Irwin, who was shortly to join General Washington's army:

TARBOROUGH, 16TH JULY, 1777.

DEAR SIR,—Being extremely unwell prevented my attending at Halifax. I am now got better, and would wish your Excellency's permission to go all to the Northward to join my Regiment, as I can't promise myself any advantage I can be of to the army, staying here.

I am very sorry to inform you of too many evil persons in this and the neighboring Counties being joined in a most wicked conspiracy; but am in hopes it may be stopped, as many have come in and made all the discovery they knew of—about thirty of them made an attempt on this place, but luckily I had about twenty-five men to oppose them. I disarmed the whole and made many take the oath.

Supplies were brought to Tarboro from time to time. Being a center for the district, the Tories could have made some useful captures. For example, Robert Bignall had a considerable quantity of ammunition in his care. Colonel Irwin, on departing for the North, must have left a big supply because we read in the proceedings of the State Legislature that Mr. Robert Bignall, of Tarborough, be directed to deliver such quantities of ammunition delivered him by Colonel Irwin to the commanding officers of Edgecombe and Nash counties, or their orders, as they may occasionally require.

Reverting once more to the Tories, it is an interesting fact that not long after the outbreak of the Revolution information of an insurrection of British sympathizers was brought to Tarboro, and at a public meeting held in the town Jonas Johnston aroused the citizens to a high pitch of patriotism. He raised a band of volunteers and marched the same evening to the point of disturbance. Colonel Johnston, although a Virginian by birth, spent most of his life in Edgecombe. He was a child when his father settled in the county. Being a plain farmer, without education, his rise to fame deserves special comment. Notwithstanding educational deficiencies, Jonas Johnston filled every office in the county, both civil and military. After a speech in the General Assembly, which showed a great deal of good sense despite glaring grammatical blunders, a professional gentleman asked him "where he got his education" and the reply came back, "at the handle of the plow."

During the struggle for independence Colonel Johnston served North Carolina in the double capacity of legislator and soldier. He fought the Tories at Moore's Creek and, less than a year afterwards, was taking part in the convention that formed the State Constitution. In 1779 he went with his regiment to South Carolina and took part in the battle of Stono. Here he received a wound which, together with his already weakened condition, caused him to succumb while on his return northward. For more than a generation the soldiers who had been under his command kept alive his memory in the community on account of his care and tenderness for their welfare.

Edgecombe sent to the Provincial Congress of North Carolina, held at Hillsborough on the 20th of August, 1775, five men whose names ought to stand forth upon the pages of the county's history. These patriots, in defiance of British authority, met their fellow-delegates from the other counties of the Province and proceeded to organize for resistance. They were Robert Bignall, Henry Irwin, Duncan Lemon, Thomas Hunter and Thomas H. Hall. In the Congress of April, 1776, that declared for independence, Edgecombe was represented by William Haywood, Duncan Lemon, Elisha Battle, Henry Irwin and Nathaniel Boddie.

She sent to the Congress at Halifax, held on the 12th of November of the same year, William Haywood, Elisha Battle, Jonas Johnston, Isaac Sessums and William Horn.

Brief sketches of a few of the county's patriots should prove of value. William Haywood, whose name will be found in two of the groups just presented, was a son of Colonel John Haywood. Both father and son became prominent in Edgecombe affairs. Passing over the Colonial period we find William Haywood a member of the Committee of Safety in his district. On September 9, 1775, he was elected colonel for the county of Edgecombe. In the Congress of April, 1776, he served on several committees, the importance of which may be judged by their works. They had the various tasks of settling the military and naval accounts, of drafting a temporary Constitution and of signing paper currency. In the November Congress he was placed upon the committee on military affairs, was made chairman of the committee on privileges and elections, etc. He served in the Governor's council until August 14, 1778. The list of William Haywood's honors could be continued, but sufficient matter has been offered to prove that his figure during the Revolution occupied a place of State-wide importance.

Elisha Battle, ancestor of more than two thousand descendants, has a long list of successes to his credit. He possessed a high character and deserved prosperity. In business, religion and politics the people of Edgecombe demonstrated their appreciation of his worth. From one of the first commissioners of the town of Tarboro he gradually advanced to a wider life. Perhaps the office of justice of the peace may be said to have been the lowest rung of his ladder to fame. While the War for Independence was progressing he worked for North Carolina in the capacity of Senator from Edgecombe. His popularity reached its height in 1778, when the State Constitutional Convention made him chairman of the committee of the whole.

Thomas H. Hall, a man of natural talents and the possessor of a classical education, would have shone among his fellows if a poetical nature had not led him too frequently into the realm of imagination. Perhaps his temperament caused him to be strongly stirred during the exciting days of 1775. At any rate he represented Edgecombe when it took courage to defy established authority. He never accepted office after the first Provincial Congress, but won some eminence as a lawyer and continued to practice as long as he lived. There were frequent instances, while a trial was progressing, when his mind evolved satirical-verses instead of listening to the opposing counsel. He was quick at repartee and made many enemies on account of tactless outbursts. His poems would have formed a considerable volume, but they are doubtless lost.

Robert Bignall, a resident of Tarboro, held a number of responsible positions in the service of the State. On December 1, 1776, he sat at Kingston as a member of a military court. A year later, the legislature appointed him as a commissioner for the purpose of obtaining arms, clothing, and other necessaries for the patriots. On December 8, 1778, Governor Caswell directed him to purchase provisions. His excellency's letter contained instructions as to the kind of pork to be bought, what the hogs should weigh, how much to pay for them, etc. In 1780 he was a commissioner of trade. At the close of the year, salt became scarce. Three wagons were sent to Tarboro for this article, but Mr. Bignall wrote to the authorities that there was no public salt on any part of the Tar River worth mentioning, nor indeed anywhere else in the State under the immediate direction of the commissioners of trade.

Robert Bignall also served in the Council of State. He must have been a valuable man to the Commonwealth because sixty thousand pounds, in money, were turned over to the War Board by him as commissioner of trade, in the year 1780. He was appointed a commissioner in 1781 to purchase or borrow tobacco. One of Mr. Bignall's letters, written at Tarboro, will be appended to this outline of his Revolutionary activities in order to present the man at close range. The letter is addressed to General Jethro Sumner at camp in Warren and proceeds:

"Just after the battle at Guilford and just as General Caswell returned from Granville home we sent to Harrisburg one barrel sugar and one barrel coffee for the major-general, which did not get up before the general got home, so that I suppose it yet remains. It was directed to Major-General Caswell; you will do well to make inquiry after it and make use of it.

"We have a report from Halifax that on Tuesday week, the Marquis Delafyatt and Lord Cornwallis had an engagement, that the former had the better day; it is said that the British lost three thousand men and the Marquis thirteen hundred. If this report be true I make no doubt but you have the particulars before now. I sincerely wish you all the success you yourself can wish for and am with great esteem."

Henry Irwin left a family of infant children to fight for his country. Reference has already been made above to this patriotic son of Edgecombe, who requested the Governor to allow him to go northward so that he could join General Washington's army. . When the Revolution began, he was a merchant at Tarboro and enjoyed the comforts of a successful business man. It was double hardship for him to enlist, as he left both the joys of a family life and the ease of a home. He fell in the battle of Germantown and, at first, it was believed that his bones were lost. However, a noble son of Philadelphia, many years ago, marked a spot in the old cemetery where Henry Irwin and seven of his companions lie. The Quaker City's historic suburb is well worth a pilgrimage, especially to North Carolinians. Edgecombe's soil may not have been stained with the gore of war, but she sent forth in the far distance men whose sacrifice enables us today to speak of "the land of the free and the home of the brave."

LOUIS D. WILSON, OF EDGECOMBE

How often does one hear, "I can't remember dates!" In most cases, the person speaking has made little effort toward this end. It is true that memorizing hundreds of dates would be useless labor to those whose lives are devoted to commercial pursuits. Yet, these same business men would probably find their hours after work more enjoyable if they possessed sufficient knowledge of the world's history to occupy themselves with a helpful diversion, instead of spending their time in physical pleasure.

Certain years mean more than others to individuals. So do they to nations. So, also, to the civilized world. Let us take the year 1789. In Europe, we can see the Bastille being demolished and its fragments distributed far and wide as mementoes. One particular relic, saved by LaFayette from the destruction wrought in this opening act of the mighty French Revolution, finds its way to America.

Washington receives the key of the infamous prison and deposits it in his home at Mount Vernon. Only two months and a half before the fall of the Bastille, he has become the President of a new nation. We now recall the inauguration scene, on April 30, 1789. New York is filled with joyous patriots, who gaze with pride upon a chief magistrate of their own choice.

Down in North Carolina the news has hardly been disseminated when an event occurs which makes no impression, except in the immediate neighborhood. A child is born in Edgecombe—a son destined to serve as a shining example of self-sacrifice for his country's honor. Louis D. Wilson quietly makes his entry into the world.

At this time Edgecombe county possessed a population which laid more stress upon acquiring wealth than upon obtaining education. There were the cultured few, but the mass of the people felt the need of money, so that both the causes of learning and religion suffered. However, the hearts and minds of the citizens were sound, and their neglect of spiritual and mental development may be attributed largely to indifference.

In 1787, the State Legislature had met in Tarboro, which circumstance speaks well for the town. Four years later, Washington spent the night there and specially mentioned in his diary Tarboro's reception of his party. He said that he was received by as good a salute as could be given by one piece of artillery; also, on the next day, that a number of most respectable inhabitants accompanied him part of the way to Greenville. The Father of his Country noted that the town was more lively and thriving than Halifax. He noted, too, the exports—corn, pork and tar. In 1803, Bishop Francis Asbury complains of the worldliness of its citizens, who had more wealth than religion. Thus we get an insight into the life of the community.

As the county seat reflected the doings of the people in general, we may assume Louis D. Wilson received only the rudiments of an education and then went to work. Wheeler's Reminiscences state he was rather a student of men than of books and add the fact of his success in business.

The date of Louis D. Wilson's entry into public life ought to be easily remembered. He first served in the lower branch of the General Assembly of North Carolina, during the year 1815. Students of history will at once think of Andrew Jackson's victory at New Orleans and Napoleon Bonaparte's defeat at Waterloo. Sufficiently interesting were these events to awaken in any ambitious breast an ardent desire to participate in larger affairs.

Throughout almost an entire generation Edgecombe's son served the State in some capacity. He remained in the House of Commons (as the lower branch was called) for five successive terms. Then he was elected to the Senate for a year. During the next three elections, he gave way to Hardy Flowers, but returned to the upper house, in 1824, for a period of nine years. When it is recalled that a term lasted for twelve months only, the popularity of Louis D. Wilson can be readily imagined.

Hardy Flowers succeeded him again in 1833. For five years the Legislature was deprived of Wilson's services, but not the State. He sat in the Constitutional Convention of 1835, before which many matters of importance were ably discussed. The most brilliant minds that could be gathered within the confines of North Carolina, debated on measures of absorbing interest.

After the Convention of 1835, members were elected to the Legislature for a term of two years. Thomas H. Hall, who had represented his district in eight United States Congresses, received the honor of being Edgecombe's first Senator under the new law. How few men today would be willing to close their career, following sixteen years of service in national councils, as a State Senator! Thomas H. Hall, friend of John Randolph, of Roanoke, accepted the honor and voted against North Carolina's reception of any portion of the surplus revenue from the United States Treasury.

Louis D. Wilson succeeded Dr. Hall in 1838, and continued to hold office until he asked leave of absence to fight for his country. During this period of nine years in the Senate, he became a favorite and won the sobriquet of the Chesterfield of that body. In 1842, he was chosen Speaker. Before passing to the dramatic climax of his life, it is worth while to add that his name was on the electoral ticket of 1836 and, as an elector, he voted for Martin Van Buren.

Niles' National Register, published at Baltimore (issue of September 4, 1847), informs its readers under the caption "War With Mexico":

"We are deeply pained to learn of the death of Colonel Wilson, of the Twelfth Infantry. He was represented to us by the last arrival as convalescent, but he died the evening of the 12th instant. He was to have commanded the train which left Vera Cruz on the 7th instant. He was buried on the 13th instant, the following orders having been issued for the occasion:

"ORDER No. 34.

"Headquarters, Vera Cruz, Aug. 12, 1847.

"It is announced to this command the melancholy intelligence of the death of Colonel Louis D. Wilson of the 12th Regiment U. S. Infantry, who died on this date.

"The escort for his funeral will be commanded by the Lieutenant Colonel commanding, and consist of the 1st U. S. infantry, stationed in the city. The funeral will take place at 5 o'clock P. M. tomorrow, to which all the U. S. navy, citizens and strangers are respectfully invited to attend.

"By order of Lieut. Col. Miles.

"W. L. CRITTENDEN, Act. Adj."

The publication, mentioned above (issue October 2nd), quotes from the Washington Union:

"We learn, that by his will, the late Colonel Louis D. Wilson, of the twentieth [sic] infantry, bequeathed to the chairman of the county court of Edgecombe in North Carolina, and to his successors in office, forty thousand dollars, to be applied to the support of the poor of said county. This act of charity is touchingly beautiful. Colonel Wilson had for years represented the county of Edgecombe in the Senate of his native State. When it appeared probable that the requisition for volunteers made by the President on the Governor of North Carolina would not be met, he resigned his seat in the Senate, volunteered, and was elected a captain, the highest post to which the voice of his men could elevate him and in that humble rank marched to Mexico. Before marching he made his will, and evinced his gratitude to the constituency which had so long honored him with their confidence, and his charitable regard for his poor neighbors, by this munificent bequest. There has not fallen in the service of his country a braver or a better man."

North Carolinians have recognized the worth of Colonel Wilson, but they probably have never read an appreciation of him by strangers. The two extracts, just noted, cannot fail to awaken a degree of pride in the breasts of all loyal citizens who recall how the white-haired patriot, of nearly sixty, left his seat of dignity to participate in the hardships of the army. Here was a man! The United States had been brought into war with Mexico but political parties were divided as to its necessity. North Carolina, among other States, hesitated about furnishing troops. Louis D. Wilson saw his duty and saved the State's honor. He aroused the men of Edgecombe and, having formed a company of volunteers, was the first to offer his services to the Governor. His patriotism awakened North Carolina.

His career in the United States Army was short, but he made his mark. On the 5th of January, 1847, he became a captain of volunteers; on March 3rd, he was given the rank of Colonel, and on April 9th, the Twelfth Infantry was placed under his command. A man of his age, unaccustomed to the Mexican climate, would be expected to feel the change from the delightful temperature of Edgecombe to the unhealthy lowlands of the Tropics. He sacrificed himself for his country.

A monument on the Town Common, at Tarboro, stands as a constant reminder to all passers-by that Edgecombe had a son who "led all the rest" in his day. The State, to its glory be it said, formed the county of Wilson, part of which was carved from old mother Edgecombe. When the Senate bade him farewell, Louis D. Wilson departed with the possession of their deep regard. How they felt is expressed in the following resolution, passed without dissent:

"Whereas, the Senate has been informed that one of its members is about to leave the halls of legislation, in North Carolina, to assume the more arduous and perilous duties of the camp and the battlefield, as commander of the volunteer companies from Edgecombe; and, whereas, no difference of opinion as to the commencement of the existing war between the United States and the Republic of Mexico should induce members of this body to withhold an expression of the opinion they entertain as to the self-sacrificing and patriotic conduct of the Senator referred to.

"Be it therefore unanimously resolved by the Senate of North Carolina now in session, that, in separating from their fellow-member, the Honorable Louis D. Wilson, Senator from Edgecombe, with whom many members of this body have been associated for years in the Senate chamber, they cannot withhold the expression of their high sense of his able, dignified, and patriotic services as a member of the Senate, and further, to express the conviction that in the more arduous and hazardous duties of the battlefield he will be no less distinguished for patriotism, courage, and never-failing devotion to the cause of his country."— *From the North Carolina Review.*

ANDREW JOHNSON, AS HE REALLY WAS

To the Editor (of the News and Observer):

I read with pleasure your suggestion that the North Carolina delegation ought to urge the next Congress to make an appropriation to build a monument in Raleigh to Andrew Johnson. The people of the United States, generally, and I am impelled to add, the people of North Carolina, particularly, know little of Abraham Lincoln's successor as Chief Executive of a troubled nation. Your long editorial article was entertaining, but more than this, it was instructive. North Carolinians should know the true Andrew Johnson.

Two years ago it was my good fortune to visit Greeneville, Tenn. The mere fact of a former President of the United States having once lived in this town would have excited my curiosity to see whatever memorials remained and to learn from the inhabitants any facts of his life, gathered, either through personal experience, or from tradition. However, I must confess that Andrew Johnson had interested me little up to this time. His service to the South, in attempting to stand against the horrors of Reconstruction had not been impressed upon my mind. But, I did remember that he had fallen into disfavor and narrowly missed disgrace.

Human beings are so constituted that they differ to a surprising degree. Stonewall Jackson's Valley campaign was an extraordinary event in military history, but I doubt seriously if the Northern teacher thinks it worth while to lay stress upon the Southerner's movements. Although the great Confederate general advanced against four Federal Armies in turn, I dare write the average Northerner possesses little knowledge thereof and would attempt to minimize Jackson's movements, if a Southern man endeavored to enlighten him.

My reason for introducing the preceding paragraph is to show how a child may receive erroneous impressions which will cling to him during his entire life. School histories, for many years following the War Between the States, were written by those who were more or less prejudiced against the South. Therefore, wrong ideas have been implanted. Both sides are revising their opinions. The descendants of Confederates and Federals need to revise their opinions of the official acts of Andrew Johnson. He was opposed to Secession, but he was also opposed to the fanatical policy of unreasoning Northerners. His power of speech won many men over to the Union side, but his sense of right did not desert him. He knew that the advocates of States' rights had hearts and intellects. He intended to act honorably. We, of today, can review his act impassionately.

I talked to a number of East Tennesseans who knew Andrew Johnson personally. They were poor men and uneducated. I wanted to know how he had impressed his humble neighbors. Without exception, the replies indicated respect. One old man told me that Johnson was always the same to everybody, that he was free from ostentation and that honors heaped upon him did not make him forget to be kind to the humblest citizen. Another said he had heard Greeneville's most distinguished citizen make a speech, at the outbreak of hostilities, which caused him to take the Union side.

I saw the old house where he worked at the tailor's trade. The sign, made by himself, was still above the door. It was crude and bore the simple inscription, A. Johnson. Mr. Patterson, his grandson, received me at the much more pretentious home where Andrew Johnson lived after he had achieved fame. The table, on which he worked as a tailor, was pointed out; also, several other relics of interest came to my notice, but mention of them would be out of place in this communication.

Raleigh can be proud of her native son. Although he adopted Tennessee, he belongs to North Carolina. The former has a right to claim him but his filial love was due the latter. Tennessee has honored Andrew Johnson, who proved worthy of his second love. Will North Carolina show appreciation of a man whose name will become brighter on the pages of history because he had the courage of his convictions, in spite of overwhelming hostility? Will she erect a statue to Andrew Johnson?

WHEN TARBORO WAS INCORPORATED

Many silent lessons are to be acquired from one page of an old book.

When I first learned that there was in the possession of the Register of Deeds of Edgecombe a plat of the town of Tarboro, as originally "laid off" in 1760, I did not lose much time in making a special note of it. A number of visits were then paid to the vault where the records are kept and a careful study was made of page 524, Book D, which contains the Plat just referred to, with the lots, streets, bounds, common, etc., as laid out by order of the Rev. James Moir, Lawrence Toole great-great-great-grandfather of Frank Powell, the present Editor of the Southerner (1910), Aquilla Sugg, Elisha Battle, and Benjamin Hart, its first Commissioners.

Anyone, who examines this Plat, must give considerable allowance for educational deficiencies, to-wit: Lawrence is spelled Lawrance, Hart is written Heart, Moire instead of Moir, lotts for lots, and commons for common; but in simply stating that similar errors occur frequently in recording the Deeds of Edgecombe of this period, I desire to call attention to the fact that the Colonial Records are peppered with mistakes in spelling. Although orthographers were few, the inhabitants possessed good sense, and after all, the state of the Province required rather men of sound judgment than erudite College graduates.

My article on the Town Common noted the fact of the corporation being bounded on three sides by public land. To be explicit, the Common included all the town property along the river bank, also the land contiguous to Holly's or Hendrick's Creek, and the present Common, beyond which looking toward the depot was "in the country."

Main Street, as we know it today, was intended to be residential. The founders evidently expected business to be conducted on Trade Street, whence the name.

There were one hundred and twenty-one lots, of half an acre each, the names of the owners being given on the opposite page to that containing the Plat. Each lot is numbered and the interested individual can thus easily learn the original owner.

Often have I wondered why the streets of Tarboro were named after the saints. One of the silent lessons, acquired from carefully studying the plat, has thrown an abundance of light on the subject.

Considering the character of two, at least, of the first Board of Aldermen, I feel safe in saying that sacred nomenclature would appeal strongly to Rev. James Moir and Elisha Battle.

Running parallel with Holly's or Hendrick's Creek, there were six streets: Creek, through which the Atlantic Coast Line now runs, Trade, St. George, now called Main, St. Andrew, St. Patrick, and St. David.

As the Province of North Carolina belonged to England, it was natural to look back upon Great Britain and Ireland for names. Therefore, a light flashed across my mind when I saw that Main Street was designated as St. George.

I said to myself, "Here they are in order one after other: St. George, first, the patron saint of England; St. Andrew, second, the patron saint of Scotland; St. Patrick, third, the patron of Ireland, and St. David, fourth, of little Wales."

The five crosstown streets between the Tar and the present Common were named as we know them in 1909: Granville, Pitt, St. James, Church and St. John.

It was natural for the Commissioners to honor Lord Granville, who owned such a big portion of the Colony.

But the most timely and appropriate name given was Pitt, for the Great Commoner who one year before had attained a position of extraordinary influence on account of the English victories by land and sea. In 1759 Pitt succeeded in choosing men who were unusually successful in every part of the globe where Frenchmen could be found.

During this year, when William Pitt, the Elder, was at the zenith of his power, his son, destined to be a great man like himself, was born; Wolfe took Quebec and consequently Canada; at Minden, in Westphalia, the Anglo-Hanoverian forces defeated the French; and Hawks crushed the French fleet off Brest.

Therefore, when Tarboro was incorporated in 1760, William Pitt probably occupied a bigger place in the minds of the inhabitants of the Province than any man in the civilized world.

Mere mention of the Court of St. James causes one to think of England and, although the palace of St. James is no longer occupied by the sovereign, it gives its name officially to the British court.

In naming St. James Street the loyal subjects looked upward but, in the case of St. John, they chose the appellation of John the Baptist, who from an early date was regarded in the Mother Country as the patron saint of the common people.

Rev. James Moir, sent out from England by the Society for The Propagation of The Gospel, was not a native American. He spent a number of years in the southern part of the Province before coming to Edgecombe county.

According to Clement Hall, a brother missionary, James Moir began his work in Edgecombe Parish about Easter, 1747.

Governor Gabriel Johnston, a man unpopular with the inhabitants of the Colony as he was unpractical and tried to mould affairs the way he wanted them, said that Mr. Moir left the southern part of the Province without asking leave of anybody.

If his Excellency had taken the trouble to inquire, he would have learned that the unfortunate Missionary had complained of the unsatisfactory conditions in the District as far back as 1742.

After preaching more than four years without proper assistance, he wrote to the Secretary of the Society and told him that his health was such that he felt the need of going to a colder climate and higher land.

Without entering into the mass of data wherein the ungodly condition of the people in the Cape Fear District is set forth, it is enough to state that the Secretary of the Society wrote to Governor Johnston about the difficulties under which Mr. Moir labored.

Whether the Missionary came to Edgecombe with or without permission, he had resided there thirteen years when Tarboro was incorporated and the fact of his being chosen one of the first Commissioners shows that the people thought something of him.

Lawrence Toole married Sabra Irwin, a sister of Henry Irwin, the Tarboro merchant who during the Revolution sacrificed himself for his country.

Henry Irwin Toole, the first, son of the Commissioner and Sabra Irwin, like his Uncle Henry Irwin also received a commission in the Continental regular army. He died early in life but successfully served his term of enlistment, after which he returned to Tarboro and entered the mercantile business.

He left three children: Henry Irwin Toole, the second; Arabella, and Mary.

Henry Irwin Toole, the second, married Ann Blount, daughter of Governor William Blount, of Tennessee. His children were Henry Irwin Toole, the third, and Mary Eliza, who married Dr. Joshua Lawrence.

Arabella Toole, the granddaughter of the Commissioner and sister of Henry Irwin Toole, second, married the Hon. James West Clark, whose house stood at the corner of Church and St. Patrick streets, on the site now occupied by the residence of his grandson, John W. Cotten.

James West Clark is buried in Calvary churchyard near his son, Henry Toole Clark.

The descendants of Edgecombe's war Governor, Henry Toole Clark, are too well known to be given here.

Mary Toole, sister of Henry Irwin Toole,

the second, and Arabella Toole married Theophilus Parker and had six children: Rev. John Haywood Parker; Catherine C., married first John Hargrave and second Rev. Robert B. Drane; Elizabeth T., married Rev. Jos. Blount Cheshire, father of the present bishop; Mary W., married first Frank Hargrave and second Governor Henry Toole Clark; Colonel Francis M. Parker, and Arabella C., whom so many of us know affectionately.

Miss Bella Parker is probably the oldest native of Tarboro alive today and the writer fervently hopes that God will spare her for many years to come.

Elisha Battle, one of the original Commissioners of the town of Tarboro, was the progenitor of the vast family in North Carolina that bears his name. Dr. Kemp P. Battle credits him with over two thousand descendants.

He was born in Nansemond County, Virginia, January 9, 1723, and at the age of twenty-five moved to Edgecombe. The attractive terms offered by the agents of Lord Granville perhaps was the cause that induced the young man to purchase the rich bottom lands along Tar River. With him came his wife, Elizabeth Sumner, first cousin of General Jethro Sumner of Revolutionary fame, and their two children. Part of his descendants still own the land he bought. However, it is well to add that he constantly purchased attractive offerings in other parts of the County.

About the year 1764, Elisha Battle joined the Baptist Church at the Falls of Tar River and continued in full fellowship. He served for twenty-eight years as Deacon until he resigned on account of age. He sometimes acted as moderator at the Associations which he usually attended and was known to be a remarkably pious, zealous member, always plain and candid in censuring and reproving vice or folly in all their shapes.

About 1756 he was appointed a Justice of the Peace and continued in that office until 1795, when he resigned.

Simply to recount the many capacities in which he served the County and Commonwealth would be enough to demonstrate the exceptional usefulness of Elisha Battle, as a statesman.

He was chosen to represent Edgecombe in the General Assembly, being elected the first time in 1771, and continued to serve for twenty years when he was compelled to resign on account of his advanced state in life.

Before a permanent seat of government for the State was selected, the General Assembly used to ballot at each session for the next temporary capital.

It was probably due to the influence of Elisha Battle, who took a prominent part in the deliberations at Fayetteville in 1786, that the Senate decided to select Tarboro as its next place of meeting.

Accordingly, the General Assembly met "at Tarborough on the nineteenth day of November, in the year of our Lord, One Thousand, seven hundred and Eighty-seven and, of the Sovereignty and Independence of the said State the Twelfth, it being the first session of this Assembly."

As evidence of the nomadic character of the legislators, I shall reproduce from the State Records (*) a Resolution passed Tuesday, December 18, 1787:

"That Harry Jones, of Edgecombe County, be allowed the sum of fifteen pounds for carrying a Copy of the Journal of last Assembly to the public printer at Fayetteville, and carting from thence to Tarborough the papers of the Senate; that the Treasurer pay him the same and be allowed."

Not only was Elisha Battle a Justice of the Peace and Legislator during the stormy Revolutionary period but he attended almost all the State Conventions, being a delegate to the State Congress of April, 1776, which authorized the North Carolina members of the Continental Congress to vote for independence, also a member of the State Congress that met

*Vol. XX, page 438.

at Halifax in November and December of the same year, which adopted the Declaration of Rights and Constitution.

When the Convention of 1788 met for deliberation of the Federal Constitution, the body showed its appreciation of his worth by appointing him chairman of the Committee of the Whole.

The latter part of his life was spent in quietude.

From a work entitled, A Concise History of the Kehukee Baptist Association, by Elders Lemuel Burkitt and Jesse Read, printed by A. Hodge at Halifax, 1803, I shall quote the following:

"In 1799 he requested his youngest son to come and take possession of the land and plantation whereon he lived (which he had before made him a deed for) that he might give up the care of a family and live with him. About this time he desired his children to meet him so that he might have private discourse with them and concluded to have his will written and execute it, although he had for many years kept a written one by him, altering it when he found it necessary. He divided his property among his children, only reserving a sum of money and notes, as security for himself. Soon after he was taken more unwell than usual. Without the least doubt of future felicity," he passed away the 6th of March, 1799, preceding George Washington, his great chieftain, by only nine months.

Jacob, the youngest son of Elisha Battle, who was called by his father, shortly before his death to come and take possession of the plantation, lived on the Cool Spring Farm, about half a mile from his father's residence, at a settlement called Old Town.

At this settlement was born James Smith Battle, his son, who possessed the distinction of adding to his inherited estate so many thousands of acres that he was able to ride from the present town limits of Rocky Mount to Tarboro almost without having to leave his own land.

His vast holdings were divided among his children.

William Smith Battle, Edgecombe's Grand Old Man, is a son of James Smith Battle and, consequently, the great grandson of Elisha Battle.

He was born October 4, 1823, and attended the Stony Hill and Louisburg Academies. He entered the university in 1840 and graduated in 1844, being well liked and noted for his manly bearing and perfect truthfulness.

At an early age he married Elizabeth M., daughter of Francis L. Dancy, the wedding taking place on July 25, 1845.

When his father purchased the Rocky

Mount Cotton Mills, one of the first factories in the State, he turned over the management to young William, who gave up his turpentine business in which he was extensively engaged.

The son, however, possessed a great deal of energy because he not only continued to plant cotton but also became manager and part owner of the Rocky Mount flour and grist mill.

Several fires, seven of which took place within two years at the Falls, and on different plantations, caused a loss of at least sixty thousand dollars above insurance.

He rebuilt both his cotton and grist mills at great expense and was on the road to success when the panic of 1873 occurred. His failure was due to low prices for manufactured products and the expense of rebuilding when materials and the rate of interest were high.

As if this were not enough, he has been afflicted with frightful loss in his family. A visit to the Battle section in the Episcopal churchyard, where his only daughter and several sons lie buried, shows mutely how heavily the hand of the Almighty has fallen upon him.

The manner in which he has borne his losses is well told by Dr. Kemp P. Battle, who writes:

"He attributed his losses to accident or the act of God. No one has ever heard him complain with bitterness of the hardness of fortune. The same high-toned, equable, kindly temper, the same tenderness of soul, which characterized him in his prosperous days, he retains when his energies are confined to a smaller area and when he is dealing with lesser interests."

William S. Battle has been little in public life. He has served as a justice of the peace and a member of the special committee whicn presided in the County Court.

He was a member of the Secession Convention that met in 1861. During the War Between the States he gave liberally of his means to the Cause.

Today he stands for the Old School and is one of the few left to remind us of Southern civilization as it existed in the ante-bellum period.

OUR TOWN COMMON

Few towns of the size of Tarboro, in North Carolina or adjacent States, can boast of a public park comparable to its Common. The present extent is only a fraction of what was originally set apart for municipal uses, and, if the future City Fathers are wise, they will refuse to part with another foot of the ground now devoted exclusively to outdoor activities of the citizenry.

When Tarboro was "laid off," in 1760, it contained only one hundred and fifty acres, but about fifty of these, bounding the corporation on three sides, were designated for the use of the town. Today Greater Tarboro covers many times the original area, yet that portion, distinctively known as the Common, appears small in comparison with the former acreage. True it is that the town owns a great deal of the land along the river bank; however, unless the unsightliness of much of the surrounding property is eliminated, the incongruity of a park, located there, would be glaring. Nature has favored the banks of the Tar, and anyone who stands on the county bridge during the summer when the growth of foliage has attained its maximum can verify this assertion.

Discriminating eyes force the onlooker to the conclusion that Nature is more beautiful than Art.

In studying the development of public squares, or commons, I desire to call attention to the MARK of mediaeval times, defined by the Century Dictionary, as a tract of land, during the middle ages in England, and Germany, belonging in common to a community of freemen, who divided the cultivated portion of ARABLE MARK among their individual members; used the COMMON or ORDINARY MARK together for pasturage or other general purposes; and dwelt in the VILLAGE MARK or central portion, or apart on their holdings.

J. Fiske, in his American Political Ideas, page 40, says: "The pleasant green COMMONS (notice that the letter 's' is added to denote the plural) on squares which occur in the midst of towns and cities in England and the United States most probably originated from the coalescence of adjacent mark-communities, whereby the border-land used in common by all was brought into the centre of the aggregate."

Referring again to the Century Dictionary, I find that the word COMMON is first set down as an adjective, and means, of or pertaining to all—that is, to all the human race, or to all in a given country, region or locality; and, secondly, as a noun (note the singular form), meaning a tract of ground, the use of which is not appropriated to an individual, but belongs to the public or to a number.

The tendency of local urban residents persistently to pluralize COMMON in speaking or writing of Tarboro's public park comes from the influence of uneducated negro servants whose perverted English made a more or less permanent imprint upon the white population.

Frequently, I have noticed the uneducated negro's habit, without any apparent reason, of adding the letter 's' to words used neither in a plural nor possessive sense. Whatever the cause, it is a patent peculiarity.

There is in Barton Heights, a suburb of Richmond, Virginia, a thoroughfare by the name of Luck Avenue. One day I was amused by a negro who asked me to direct him to Luck's Avenue. Even as I write, I can hear the Edgecombe name Sugg lengthened to Suggs. It was pronounced in this manner by a young man, a former pupil of the Tarboro High School.

Here in Tarboro one hears Zanders so often that, if my maternal grandfather, Zander (whose praenomen I received one week after birth), was alive today and could mingle with the citizens of town and county as was his wont thirty-odd years ago, he would be tempted to follow the prevailing fashion.

Through the kindness of that genial gentleman and efficient official, Clerk John A. Weddell, there lies before me a typewritten copy of the Acts of the General Assembly in relation to the Town of Tarboro.

In order to support my contention that the correct usage of COMMONS applies only to the plural, when one refers to land devoted to public purposes, section one, of the Act passed November 30, 1760, for establishing a town on the land of Joseph Howell on Tar River, herewith follows:

"1. WHEREAS it hath been represented to this Assembly, that the land of Joseph Howell, lying on the South side of Tar River, in Edgecombe county, is a healthy, pleasant situation, well watered, and commodious for trade and commerce: and James Moir, Lawrence Tool, Aquilla Sugg, Elisha Battle and Benjamin Hart, have contracted with the said Joseph Howell for the purchase of one hundred and fifty acres of the said land, and have accepted and taken a deed of feoffment for the aforesaid one hundred and fifty acres from the said Joseph Howell, and caused the same to be laid off in lots and streets, and also a part thereof for a COMMON (note the singular form), for the use of the said town, and have sold a great number of the said lots of half an acre each to sundry persons, who are desirous that a town shall be established thereon, for promoting the trade and navigation of the said river."

On the 18th of November, 1786, in support of my claim I find evidence in the Act that passed the General Assembly entitled, "An act to establish the late survey and plan of the town of Tarboro, as made and laid down by the direction of the Commissioners composing the body politic and corporate of the said town, and to amend an act entitled, 'An Act for The Better Regulation of The Town of Tarboro.'

"WHEREAS it is represented to this General Assembly, that from the irregular manner in which most of the buildings first erected in the town of Tarboro have been placed, as well as to prevent in future the erecting of others in like manner, it hath been judged advisable by the inhabitants of the said town generally, that the width of the streets thereof, should be curtailed and their limits fixed with, precision, and it being further represented that pursuant thereto the Commissioners have caused an accurate survey of the said town and TOWN COMMON," etc.

Sufficient data have been produced to prove conclusively that Tarboro's public park should be called the TOWN COMMON and, not the COMMONS.

Let us return to the COMMON itself and ask ourselves whether the citizens, as a whole, appreciate it? Will they organize a Civic Improvement League and beautify the park?

By removing the Louis D. Wilson monument from the Court House yard to its present position and in the erection of the Confederate memorial through the untiring efforts of the patriotic daughters of Edgecombe, steps have been taken in the right direction.

The writer hopes that at no distant day the present [1909] wooden school structures, unsymmetrical and ill to look upon, will be supplanted by one modern building, durable, fireproof and sanitary. If he be allowed to hope further, the new schools will not be built on the Common, but from Lloydfield to Hilma will be an unobstructed stretch of landscape, save where the stately oaks tower.

Adorn it with flowers and rare shrubs to develop a sense of the beautiful. George Henry Lewes, in his Problems of Life and Mind, says, "Beauty, if it does not take precedence of utility, is certainly coeval with it."

A love of the beautiful also awakens a higher moral feeling, as Lowell tells us: "Comparative criticism teaches us that moral and esthetic defects are more nearly related than is commonly supposed."—*From The Southerner.*

REMINISCENT, BIOGRAPHICAL, AND GENEALOGICAL

During the summer of 1892 my uncle, Gus Zander, took me with him on a tour, which included the Middle Atlantic States, New England and Canada, our most northern point being Quebec.

Older citizens of Tarboro may remember the extraordinary rainfall in June and the first part, at least, of July. We left for Old Point on the 5th of the latter month and had rain for a companion from the time we stepped upon the train until our arrival at Pinner's Point.

As a child, I used to listen to discussion on all kinds of topics. The late Thomas E. Lewis was bookkeeper for my father at this time. He, like others in town and country, joined in comment on the topic then of uppermost importance. Among the reasons advanced for the unusual amount of rain, he gave an old superstition, belief in which I do not credit him with, but many people did believe it once upon a time.

Mr. Lewis offered in explanation of the continued "wet season" that, if it rained on St. Swithin's Day, it would rain for forty days thereafter, probably supposing the day to be in June.

Swithin, or Swithun, was a Bishop of Winchester, Hampshire, England, from 852 to 862 A. D. He was a tutor to Egbert's son, Ethelwulf, and was noted for building churches, a man of piety and humility. He also performed miracles, according to one or more of his chroniclers.

A sample of this power happened thus. While superintending the building of a bridge at the east side of the city, he one day saw some of his workmen break an old woman's basket of eggs, whereupon the bishop miraculously restored them.

Before his death he asked to be laid where "passers by might tread on his grave, and where rain from the eaves might fall on it."

He was buried in the churchyard at Winchester. A century later he was canonized, and the monks exhumed his body to deposit it in the cathedral.

This translation was to have taken place on the 15th of July, but, owing to violent rains, it was delayed. Hence the belief that forty days of rainy or clear weather will ensue, if the 15th of July is rainy or fair.

While in Montreal, I received a letter from my school teacher, Mr. Wilkinson. It shows so well his power of interesting the small boy, and even grown-ups, by his variety of detail, that, although he complains of being too "jaded and drowsy" under the circumstances to write a worthy letter, I shall quote a liberal portion of it on account of the many things he has touched upon and his happy manner of expression:

TARBORO, N. C., July 23, 1892.

DEAR GASTON,—After five days' absence from Tarboro, and after traveling by buggy about one hundred and eighty miles through the southern part of our County visiting the public schools, nothing, on my arrival home this evening, greeted me more pleasantly than your very interesting letter, and my only regret is that my tired and wearied condition tonight will not let me indite to you an interesting letter in return for yours. My arrival here this evening was not early enough to gather the news, or town gossip, but on my way home from the postoffice I saw your mother across the street, yet I was too much jaded then to cross over and speak to her. She was looking well, very well. Your little sister was behind her looking as rosy and as sweet as usual. * * *

The Tarboro Baseball Club has had two or three match games, and, I hear—always came out victorious, but my information on such subjects is very limited, being in the country for several days, and in company with farmers only, my head is well-nigh filled with something about corn, cotton, peanuts, rice, tobacco, and even "Third Party," all somewhat mixed and confused with public schools, redbugs, mosquitoes, etc., which will probably disturb my dreams tonight but will not likely interest you.

I discovered that Daniel, the painter, was applying his paint brush to our old school building, trying to put on a newer, gayer dress, ready for our reception, the 29th of August.

The hot suns of July are upon us, but with them come the delicious peach and the sweet melon, the delight of the small boy who now begins to neglect his bat and ball for the more pleasant retreats on the shady banks of Hendrick's Creek or the Tar.

I am too jaded and drowsy tonight to write a letter worthy of demanding one moment of your attention from those grand objects which Nature has showered upon the banks of the St. Lawrence and its tributaries where your mind may feast and look up through "Nature to Nature's God."

Your deeply interested friend,
F. S. WILKINSON.

Those who used to be lovers of the National Game in the early nineties, may recall the locally celebrated baseball team, referred to above, whose twirler of the sphere, now Dr.

R. H. Johnston, was looked upon as a wonder by the small boys.

I recall reading the Weekly Southerner, sent to us at Montreal, how Washington came up to Tarboro with the famous Kugler, so the newspaper stated, and expected to show our boys the art of ball playing. Then followed an account of a game during the first part of which things did not look well for Tarboro but, as Artie Morris said, Dick Johnston had not warmed up yet.

When he did warm up, Washington ceased her hitting and run getting. At the end of the seventh inning, the score was five to five. Tarboro got a batting streak and made five runs both in the eighth and ninth innings.

I was informed on my return that Luther Bryan gave vent to his feelings of joy, when the last ball had been pitched, by holding it up in his mitt and exclaiming: "Fifteen to Five in favor of Tarboro."

Mr. Wilkinson taught me from September, 1890, to February, 1895, a period of four years and a half. I began in one of the low classes and, when I left, Dolph Staton* and myself composed the highest class of the school. If Dolph is ever called upon to fight for his country and is as persistent and patient in demanding the Surrender of the enemy as he used to be in demanding it of his schoolmates

---

*Now Commander with a creditable war record.

at the Tarboro Male Academy, the United States Navy may be overwhelmed, but it will never give up the battle.

I spent a pleasant evening with "Old Frank" during my visit to Tarboro, a year ago (1909). We talked about school days, slavery, town and county history, libraries, and other subjects of mutual interest.

Our conversation on ante-bellum Tarboro brought forth the information that he recollected Alexander W. Weddell as a young man, who I learned, since writing the sketch of his life, was born in the house on Church Street, just behind the Henry Clark Bridgers' building, now occupied by Paul McCabe.

Robert Burns Lindsay, a school teacher of Tarboro in the forties of the last century and later Governor of Alabama, claimed our attention for a while.

Mr. Wilkinson conveyed the impression that the gentleman went to Mississippi, but I was at that time not in possession of data to offer to the contrary.

The life of Mr. Lindsay ought to interest my readers as he probably taught some of their ancestors.

He was born in Lochmaben, Dumfries-shire, Scotland, July 4, 1824. He received a classical education, graduating at St. Andrews University, the oldest in Scotland and situated in a city of the same name, noted for the manufacture of golf balls, a Mecca for lovers of William H. Taft's favorite sport.

When he was eighteen years old, Robert Burns Lindsay came to America and taught school in Tarboro. For six years he acted as schoolmaster and, while supporting himself in this way, read law.

In 1848 he went to Tuscumbia, Alabama, and opened a law office.

He represented Franklin County in the General Assembly in 1853, also in the Senate in 1857, and again in 1865.

Meantime he married Sarah Miller Winston, daughter of a wealthy planter of North Alabama, and a half sister of John Anthony Winston, Alabama's first native Governor who is reported to have led the Eighth Infantry of his State at the battle of Seven Pines, with bridle reins in his teeth and a navy pistol in each hand and when at close quarters with the Northern troops being ordered to surrender, he replied that he "didn't join the army to surrender; that was not his business there."

Mrs. Lindsay was a first cousin of Governor John J. Pettus, of Mississippi, and his younger brother, United States Senator Edmund Winston Pettus, who with his colleague, John T. Morgan, represented Alabama for many years and, together was the most venerable pair in the National Senate.

In 1857, the same year he was elected for

the first time to the State Senate, Mr. Lindsay was appointed on the board of visitors to the West Point Military Academy.

He was selected, in 1860, by the Alabama Democratic Convention as a presidential elector. When the breach in the party came and two tickets were placed in the field, he refused to support the States' Rights wing under Breckenbridge and made an extensive canvas for Douglas.

But, Robert Burns Lindsay was loyal to his adopted State for, although like many native Southerners, he vigorously opposed secession, he followed the fortunes of Alabama, when she did secede, and assisted in her defence.

The fact of his being returned to the State Senate for a second term, at the close of the War Between the States, shows that the people thought well of him.

Under the Constitution of 1868, which permitted a citizen of foreign birth to hold the office of Chief Executive of Alabama, he was nominated by the Democratic Convention in 1870, and elected by a narrow margin over the Radical incumbent, Smith, who contested the result, and called in the power of the Federal army to sustain him.

After a few stormy weeks, Governor Lindsay was left in quiet possession of authority. He served during a troubled period in the history of the State, but returned to private life with unblemished character.

He was of ordinary height but stout. His deportment was polished, his appearance pleasing, and he possessed high moral and social standing. His superior information and conservative views always exercised a marked influence. He shone as a debator, being lucid both in his statements and conclusions. He was also a linguist.

When R. B. Lindsay came to Edgecombe to teach school, he was a very young man. Therefore, what I shall now impart, ought to detract nothing from the dignity of the gentleman but rather to make us feel that he belonged partly to our County, so we may speak of him as we do of homefolks.

His school was in the Town Common, on the site of the present High School building. Mr. Wilkinson, as a boy, used to see him, but did not attend his school. His recollection of R. B. Lindsay was that he taught so loudly, he could be heard to Main Street.

Miss Bella Parker told me that she could stand on her back porch and listen to his pupils recite their geography lesson. She lived with her father, Theophilus Parker, at the intersection of Church and St. Patrick streets, diagonally across from the house in which I was born.

Dorsey Battle was editor of the Southerner

at the time of my birth. He had a concise and happy manner of recording events. Bennie Brown and myself were born on the same day, December 17, 1879. A notice in the Local Column announced our entry into the world thus:

"Again the infantile cry is heard. This time R. C. Brown and D. Lichtenstein. Both boys. Congrats."

Theophilus Parker lived on what was known to me as "Old Dr. Cheshire's Lot." One of my earliest recollections is the well thereon, situated near St. Patrick Street, whither negro servants of the neighbors would make regular pilgrimages.

As a child, I occasionally attended services at the Episcopal Church, and, seeing "Old Dr. Cheshire" so often while playing both on his lot and in the neighborhood, I learned to look upon him with reverence.

My sentiment for his family has endured to this day and it is with extreme pleasure that I give an outline of his ancestry through the Blount branch, not only one of the oldest families in North Carolina but also ancient in European history; and, according to tradition, extending back to—but, wait a moment.

The Blounts (see foot note), first appear in English history in 1066, when three brothers accompanied William the Conqueror from

Normandy and fought at the battle of Hastings.

These noblemen were the sons of Blound, Lord of Guisnes, in France, who was traditionally derived from the Biondi of Italy and, to go back further descended from the Flavii of classical Rome.

The name Blound has taken various forms, for examples: le Blond, le Blont, Blunt, le Blunte, etc.

It may be regarded as a synonym of the Anglo-Saxon word White. The family probably assumed the cognomen originally on account of fair hair and a light complexion, whence the French word blond, incorporated into the English language.

After the Conquest one of the brothers returned home but the other two, Robert and William, remained and participated in a division of the spoils, the former obtaining no less than thirteen lordships in Suffolk and the latter six lordships in Lincolnshire.

The said Sir Robert le Blount, as he has been styled, was the first feudal Baron of Ixworth (the place of his residence) and Lord of Orford Castle. He married Gundreda, youngest daughter of Henry, Earl Ferrers, and had a son and heir, Gilbert le Blount, second Baron of Ixworth.

William le Blount, sixth Baron of Ixworth, who was standard bearer to Simon de Montfort, and fell at the battle of Lewes, May 14, 1264, was attainted and the Barony forfeited. He left no issue, but the representation of the family passed to his uncle, Sir Stephen le Blount, who married Maria le Blount, heiress of Saxlingham, and had two sons.

The elder, Sir Robert Blount (note now that the French article le has been dropped) who succeeded his father as heir, married Isabel, daughter and co-heir of the feudal Lord of Odinsels, by whom he acquired the manor of Belton in Rutlandshire, and had three sons.

Sir William Blount, probably the youngest, is the only one who immediately concerns us. He left a son, Sir Walter le Blount, Knight of Ockha, otherwise Rook, in the county of Warwick. Sir Walter, for some reason, temporarily revived the French article, which was also used by his elder son, Sir William le Blount.

Sir Walter, Knight, of Ockha, married Johanna, third sister and co-heir of Sir William de Sodington, and acquired the estate of Sodington, which to this day (1910) continues one of the principal seats of the head branch of the family.

His younger son, Sir John Blount, married twice. By his first wife, Isolda, he had two sons and by his second wife, Eleanor, he had one son, Sir Walter Blount, the famous companion in arms of the Black Prince.

Sir John Blount, Junior, a son of his first wife, was a direct ancestor of Sir George Blount, Knight of Sodington, who himself was father of Sir Walter Blount, created a Baronet, October 5, 1642.

This Sir Walter Blount suffered severely in the cause of Charles the First, was imprisoned at Oxford, and in the tower of London. He married Elizabeth, daughter of George Wylde, of Droitwich, County of Worcester, by whom he had four sons (all of whom, like their father, fought with the Cavaliers against the Roundheads).

He was succeeded by his eldest son, Sir George Blount, second Baronet, ancestor of the present* Sir Walter de Sodington Blount, of Sodington, county of Worcester, ninth Baronet, born December 19, 1833.

Sir Walter de Sodington Blount married Elizabeth, daughter of James Zacharias Williams and has two sons, Walter Aston (born October 9, 1876), his heir to be, and Edward Robert; also two daughters, Mary Corisande and Eva Appolonia.

He is a Deputy-Lieutenant, Justice of the Peace, was educated at Ascott, a Roman Catholic college near Birmingham, and owns about six thousand acres.

*The above article appeared on March 5, 1910.

At this point I wish to direct the reader's attention again to Sir Walter Blount who was created a Baronet in 1642. I mentioned the fact of his having four sons and, incidentally, shall add that he also had four daughters. Another thing to be recalled is that he was succeeded by his eldest son, George.

During the reign of Charles the Second, the younger sons of Sir Walter Blount emigrated to America. One settled in Virginia, the other two, James and Thomas, in North Carolina.

Their descendants are so numerous, I am compelled to confine myself to James who settled in Albemarle, in 1669. He is spoken of in contemporary documents as a member of the Governor's Council, as one of the Burgesses of Chowan, and as a leading character in the young Colony.

His son, John Blount had ten children, six daughters and four sons. John Blount's name is recorded in the Vestry Book of St. Paul's Parish, Chowan Precinct, 1701, as a member of the first vestry ever appointed in North Carolina.

John Blount, the Second, of Mulberry Hill, son of the vestryman, was prominent in civil and church matters, and his daughter married the first Bishop-elect, Dr. Charles Pettigrew.

His youngest brother, Joseph Blount, the

First, was a member of many Colonial Assemblies.

Joseph Blount, the Second, son of the Assemblyman, was a Warden of the Episcopal Church and a member of the Standing Committee of the Convention which elected Dr. Pettigrew.

Parenthetically, so to speak, it is well to state that the first effort for diocesan organization of the Protestant Episcopal Church in North Carolina was made at Tarboro in 1790, and the Centennial Celebration thereof took place in Calvary Parish, May, 1890, a notable Convention.

Joseph Blount, the Third, son of Joseph Blount, the Second, was the father of Joseph Blount, the Fourth, who died unmarried.

A daughter of Joseph Blount, the Second, married John Cheshire in 1812. His only son, Rev. Joseph Blount Cheshire, who labored over half a century for the Church, inherited the maternal family name and transmitted it to his son, the Bishop, Rt. Rev. Joseph Blount Cheshire, the Second, whose son, Joseph Blount Cheshire, the Third, represents the eighth generation in America.

The last recollection I have of "old Dr. Cheshire" will always linger in my memory as one of the most sacred moments of my life. My visit was occasioned by the desire to tell him good-bye, just previous to my departure for Europe. A warm sun that compelled the abundant shedding of clothing (it was during the early summer of 1899), bathed the face of Nature and seemed to exert its powerful influence in the beneficent task of adding a luxurious charm to the foliage of the garden, the beauty of which had been greatly enhanced by Dr. Cheshire's personal attention.

We were a group of three, Miss Kate Cheshire, his daughter, completing the picture. After a very pleasant conversation, I arose to say good-bye but the venerable old man raised his hand and Miss Kate told me her father wanted to give me his blessing. I bent my knee and received from this "Man of God," a patriarch among his people, an invocation for divine favor.

When I returned from abroad, "Old Dr. Cheshire" had been "gathered unto his fathers." He died in perfect faith that he would see God and the angels. For him the Bible was a book of doctrine, a book of morals, and a book of religion, of special revelation from God.

Foot note.—Bibliography consulted for Blount family: Lower's Dictionary of Family Names, London, 1860; Burke's Extinct Peerage, London, 1831; Burke's Peerage and Baronetage, New York and London, 1904; Who's Who, English edition, 1907; Wheeler's Reminiscences, Columbus, Ohio, 1884; and Sketches of Church History in North Carolina, Wilmington, 1892.

INDEX

SUBSCRIBERS

New York Public Library.
North Carolina State Library.
Virginia State Library.
William and Mary College Library.
Edgar A. Poe Shrine.
Albert L. Cox, Raleigh, N. C.
G. F. Ezekiel, New Orleans, La.
Rev. Frank T. McFaden, Winchester, Va.
Dr. Alfred M. Schultz, Greenville, N. C.
W. A. Powell, Baltimore.
William B. Abrams.
Robert L. Acree.
A. L. Adamson.
W. A. Aiken, Jr.
Otis M. Alfriend.
C. O. Alley.
James B. Anderson.
Wythe D. Anderson.
Carl W. Appich.
George L. Appich.
N. W. Atkinson.
Albert T. August.
Hardin K. Bache.
R. R. Bacon.
E. N. Bailey.
A. W. Baker.
G. R. Barker.
C. H. Barlow.
George S. Barnard.
A. Bartlett.
S. P. Bass.
Dr. Harry Bear.
Dr. Joseph Bear.
Nathan Bear.
Alfred Benson.
E. H. Benson.

W. L. Bernstein.
J. T. Bethel.
M. W. Beville.
George A. Blackwell.
W. H. Bontz, Jr.
Albert O. Boschen.
Barney Bowman.
H. S. Binswanger.
J. A. Branch.
Fred F. Braswell.
Herman C. Brauer.
H. Edward Briel.
Charles Briggs.
Edward W. Broidy.
I. H. Brooks.
Charles R. Brown.
F. W. Bruce.
Jonathan Bryan.
F. S. Bullington.
Charles B. Burch.
S. S. Burch, Jr.
William C. Butler.
Norman Call.
W. C. Carrick.
F. W. Carrington.
B. Cates.
A. R. Chalkley.
C. C. Chapin, Jr.
C. C. Chappell, Jr.
C. L. Chappell.
Basil I. Chapman.
George R. Childress.
A. B. Clarke.
James M. Clift.
Jesse D. Coats.
Grover C. Cocke.
Henry Cohen, Jr.
Louis Cohen.
M. J. Cohen.
Jacob S. Cohn.
H. Norman Cole.
C. H. Collier.

Julian L. Cone.
Lawson H. Cooke.
J. E. O. Cosby.
James Cowan.
J. W. Craze.
Dr. Lavinder D. Creasy.
C. C. Crouch.
S. S. Cunningham.
J. M. Culbreth.
John A. Cutchins.
Irvin L. Davis.
Vernon N. Davis.
W. A. Deitrick.
Ralph L. Dombrower.
Jay Donohue.
James C. Drinard.
Jesse C. Duke.
J. E. Dunford.
N. M. Dunford.
W. W. Dunford.
Frank H. Dunn.
Macon A. Dyson.
H. U. & F. D. Ebel.
John S. Eggleston.
Claude Elam.
William Milton Engard.
H. G. Emrick.
Jack L. Epps.
Harry L. Ewell.
J. Davis Ewell.
E. B. Farinholt.
D. H. Feldman.
Edgar H. Fergusson.
John E. Finney.
W. J. Fisher.
C. E. Flippen.
A. H. Flournoy.
A. D. Freedman.
H. Horter Fricke.
Edward L. Frost.
Edward R. Fuller.
J. S. Galeski.
Walter J. Gans.
J. Vaughan Gary.
Samuel H. Gellman.
W. C. Germelman.
Sam Gerson.
Otis W. Gilman.
H. T. Goddin.

J. Goldfin.
Aaron L. Goldwater.
James W. Gordon.
John G. Granson.
Leo Greenebaum.
Daniel Grinnan.
Aron Gross.
Barton H. Grundy.
Julian Gunn.
Henry Gunst.
James L. Hagan.
John W. Hall, Jr.
Otto Hamersley.
J. D. Hank, Jr.
H. J. Hansen.
D. H. Harden.
Charles W. Hardwicke.
Louis D. Harper.
E. M. Hastings.
Aubrey Hawkins.
L. C. Hazlegrove.
Edward M. Heller.
F. Hiram Herndon.
Robert J. Hess.
T. S. Hiteshew.
J. H. Hodes.
F. S. Holdcroft.
D. Holoman.
J. Garland Hood.
R. E. Hord.
Alvin B. Hutzler.
Henry S. Hutzler.
Maurice L. Hutzler.
Sam Iseman.
C. L. Jackson.
Herbert R. Jackson.
Willis R. Jenkins.
H. Stewart Jones.
J. H. Jones.
James P. Jones.
Otis V. Jones.
Richard W. Jones.
Jesse M. Johnson.
Thomas R. Johnson.
George Ben Johnston.
J. T. Kaempf.
Edmund Kahn.
Oscar Kahn.
Meyer Kalman.

Martin Kapiloff.
Dr. Lazarus Karp.
Carl Kaufman.
George W. Kendler.
W. J. Kendrick.
Robert Lecky, Jr.
F. Legnaioli.
R. T. Levien.
Arthur Levy.
John C. Lewis.
Joseph Lichtenstein, Sr.
Carl M. Lindner.
W. S. Lipscomb.
David London.
E. M. Long.
Benjamin Lovenstein.
Jacob Lovenstein.
Louis Lovenstein.
George W. Lowery.
J. A. Lundin.
George A. Lutto.
O. J. Mallory.
David Marks.
M. Marks.
Morton I. Marks.
M. E. Marcuse.
Eugene C. Massie.
A. L. Mattern.
Deane Maury.
Randolph Maynard.
Julian H. McCabe.
C. E. McEwen.
J. Herbert Mercer.
H. L. Melton.
Wyndham R. Meredith.
W. H. Merritt.
George H. Meyer.
Ellis Miller.
L. Calvin Miller.
E. Ross Millhiser.
Ernest D. Mills.
James A. Moncure.
Hill Montague.
R. L. Montague.
A. F. Moran.
C. H. Morrissett.
G. G. Moss.
E. B. Muire.
C. Ridgeway Moore.

Conway C. Mundy.
D. P. Mundy.
E. T. D. Myers, Jr.
Leon M. Nelson.
William Newman.
J. C. Noel.
Ravee Norris.
Rosewell Page.
David H. Parrish.
J. Scott Parrish.
William J. Parrish, Jr.
S. S. P. Patteson.
E. C. Pelouze.
C. S. Perry.
W. S. Pettit.
J. M. Pierce.
R. Dixon Powers.
J. D. Pretlow.
James H. Price.
Ordway Puller.
D. L. Pulliam.
Fred H. Powell.
J. P. Quarles.
Merrill E. Raab.
George W. Rady.
W. W. Ratcliffe.
J. Kent Rawley.
P. L. Rawlings.
E. Reams.
Elmo S. Redwood.
E. Ray Richardson.
C. W. Rex.
Richard F. Reynolds.
James A. Richardson.
George C. Richwine.
Henry C. Riely.
G. L. Riker.
William Rindsberg.
F. W. Robins.
Pell S. Rogers.
W. L. Rogers.
Louis Rosenberg.
Samuel S. Rosendorf.
H. W. Rountree.
Joseph M. Rubens.
Louis Rueger.
N. Rutenberg.
H. F. Ryder.
James F. Ryland.

J. L. Satterfield.
Charles O. Saville.
John F. Saville.
George F. Scheer.
Sol Scher.
E. F. Schmidt.
Gus M. Schwarzschild.
Henry Schwarzschild.
Sol M. Schwarzschild.
David Siegel.
Dan P. Sigourney.
G. R. Smith.
W. F. Smith.
Thomas B. Snead.
William L. Snider.
John H. Southall.
John E. Stewart.
S. G. Sterling.
Charles E. Straus, Jr.
Irving J. Straus.
M. J. Straus.
Lewis S. Strauss.
E. Strudwick.
Guy Stulting.
B. Garnett Tabb.
A. P. Taylor.
W. P. Terrell.
A. Lynn Thomas.
H. M. Thomas.
David Treger.
J. E. Trevillian.
S. S. Trevvett.
William L. Tyler.
Sol E. Ullman.
A. C. Van Pelt.
M. B. Van Doren.

Victor St. John Vaughan.
Jefferson Wallace.
Morton L. Wallerstein.
C. L. Walthall.
J. Leicester Watts.
Shepherd Webb, 5 copies.
Harold Weidenfeld.
A. I. Weinberg.
Joseph M. Weinberg.
G. Ed Weitzel.
V. A. Wells.
William C. West.
C. G. Wheatley.
Joseph F. White.
R. A. White.
John J. Wicker, Jr.
Mert A. Wilber.
A. Simpson Williams.
Berkeley Williams.
John W. Williams.
Lewis C. Williams.
A. P. Wilmer.
B. W. Wilson.
Wins Wilson.
Charles R. Winfree.
Robert E. Winfree.
John T. Wingo.
Geddes H. Winston.
Thomas S. Winston.
P. Earl Wood.
R. S. Woods.
Coleman Wortham.
Marcellus E. Wright.
W. P. Wright.
William H. Wyatt, Jr.
Marion F. Yarborough.